With this book, Aimee Byrd has done a [...] a time when society at large is questioni [...] in general and the legitimacy of friends [...] Aimee challenges her readers to test t [...] whether they are dictated by Scriptures or by culture and tradition. The answers might surprise you.

Read this book even if you think you are already the best of friends. You will find many unexpected questions and insightful recommendations. If you have children, it will help you to establish in them, from an early age, good habits of friendship and sibling relationships.

—**Simonetta Carr**, Author, *Broken Pieces and the God Who Mends Them* and the Christian Biographies for Young Readers series

Jesus was willing to break through ethnic, political, religious, and gender barriers like a wrecking ball. There was not a man-made obstacle to forgiveness and spiritual growth that he would allow to stand in his way. Aimee Byrd's book on friendship will be a rich resource for believers to consider how they might follow in Jesus' steps. Read it to help you think, reflect, and develop personal convictions for Jesus-centered relationships.

—**Dan DeWitt**, Director, Center for Biblical Apologetics and Public Christianity, and Associate Professor, Applied Theology and Apologetics, Cedarville University

Aimee Byrd's thought-provoking treatment of cross-gender friendship in the family of God is at once rich biblical theology and piercing cultural critique. Eschewing the reductionistic, fear-based, and eroticized views of the other sex that too often typify even those within the church, she answers the question "Can men and women live as sacred siblings in the church?" with an emphatic "Yes, they can—and they must!" . . . if we are to truly follow in the footsteps of our Elder Brother, Jesus Christ.

—**Michael R. Emlet**, Faculty Member, Christian Counseling and Educational Foundation; Author, *CrossTalk* and *Descriptions and Prescriptions*

Aimee has not written a rule book full of dos and don'ts for friendships between women and men in the church. She has not drawn a neat little diagram of what is and isn't allowed. What she has done is to give men and women of faith a book that answers the question of *why* there should be vibrant friendships between male and female siblings in Christ; and, in doing so, she gives us the tools to decide how this will be accomplished in a God-honoring way. Beginning at the heart of our identity as children of God, Aimee builds a strong case for why our current approach to male/female friendships misses the heart of what God has for his children.

—**Jasmine Holmes**, Blogger, jasminelholmes.com

To be honest, I hate that this book had to be written. But since it is undeniably necessary, I am so thankful that Aimee Byrd took up the task. She writes not merely from experience but with a deep theological orientation and informed pastoral concerns. She reminds Christians to be less influenced by *When Harry Met Sally...* than they are by Jesus and Paul.

Too often as Christians we actually sound no different from non-Christians in our assumptions. Why can't we—as the household of God—be courageous in our concern, affectionate in our love, and wise in our practices? Rather than being driven by fear, let's follow biblical expectations for what it means to be in the family of God.

Thankfully, Aimee calls us to be faithful siblings who are soaked in the love of the Father, strengthened by Christ our elder brother, and empowered in the Spirit of holiness. By God's grace, let us learn to live more like a healthy family.

—**Kelly M. Kapic**, Professor of Theological Studies, Covenant College, Lookout Mountain, Georgia; Author, *Embodied Hope*

The apostle Paul never called his closest associates "friends"; they were brothers and sisters in Christ. Expanding on his insight, Aimee Byrd explains friendship between males and females in the church as a sacred-siblings calling to love, sanctification, and celebration. Too many people today guard their hearts with rules motivated by fear, concern for reputation, or gross misunderstandings of who we are instead of by theology. *Why Can't We Be Friends?* ushers us into the deep spaces of Christian theology in a way that rearranges our relationships. If we will be siblings in the kingdom, it's time we accepted our future for the sake of our present. This is the best book I have seen on this subject.

—**Scot McKnight**, Julius R. Mantey Chair of New Testament, Northern Seminary, Lisle, Illinois

Have you ever wondered whether there's more that God intended for men and women to experience in their friendships with one another this side of heaven? With winsome candor, extensive research, and a vibrant love for the church, Aimee Byrd urges readers to confront the stereotypes that limit friendship between men and women by seeking above all else to *promote holiness* in one another. Her words awaken a desire to richly enjoy the brother/sister relationships to which our elder brother, Christ, calls us. Her life bears this out. Thank you, Aimee, for such a courageous and timely gift to the church!

—**Dave Myers**, Elder, New Hope Orthodox Presbyterian Church, Frederick, Maryland

In our hyper-sexualized culture, there is a very real danger that the church will unconsciously allow the world to set her priorities, if only by way of overreaction, and will thereby ironically lose sight of important aspects of biblical teaching. Nowhere is this more likely than in the sphere of relationships between the sexes. Thus, Aimee Byrd's plea for a recovery of such friendships in the church, through the rediscovery of the significance of the biblical use of sibling language, is timely. The church is to be a place of love and hospitality where we are to take seriously the transformation of our identities in Christ. A provocative but irenic breath of fresh air on a contentious topic, this book shows how we can and should do that. Highly recommended.

—**Carl R. Trueman**, William E. Simon Visiting Fellow in Religion and Public Life, Princeton University; Professor of Biblical and Religious Studies, Grove City College

Too often, Christians swear allegiance to the cultural belief that platonic relationships between the sexes are unthinkable. In the interest of avoiding adultery at all costs, we segregate men and women from one another within the church. But *one another* is precisely what we lose when this is the case. Aimee Byrd calls us back to the Bible's vision of believers as the family of God—a family of spiritual brothers and sisters who actually believe they are capable of and called to loving *one another* deeply, from the heart (see 1 Peter 1:22). I can't think of a more countercultural message or a more compelling witness to the gospel than a church marked by men and women who trade the fear of adultery for the freedom of appropriate sibling friendships as they partner to advance the kingdom. Aimee shows us this better way.

—**Jen Wilkin**, Bible Teacher; Author, *Women of the Word* and *None Like Him*

WHY CAN'T
WE BE FRIENDS?

AVOIDANCE IS NOT PURITY

AIMEE BYRD

PUBLISHING
P.O. BOX 817 • PHILLIPSBURG • NEW JERSEY 08865-0817

Library of Congress Cataloging-in-Publication Data

Names: Byrd, Aimee, 1975- author.
Title: Why can't we be friends? : avoidance is not purity / Aimee Byrd.
Description: Phillipsburg : P&R Publishing, 2018.
Identifiers: LCCN 2018016375 | ISBN 9781629954172 (pbk.) | ISBN 9781629954189 (epub) | ISBN 9781629954196 (mobi)
Subjects: LCSH: Man-woman relationships--Religious aspects--Christianity. | Friendship--Religious aspects--Christianity. | Sex--Religious aspects--Christianity.
Classification: LCC BT705.8 .B97 2018 | DDC 261.8/357--dc23
LC record available at https://lccn.loc.gov/2018016375

To my biological siblings,
Luke, Brooke, Eli, and Brody.
Being your big sister has shaped me
and all my other relationships.
And it's been one of my greatest honors in life.
Praise God that you are my spiritual siblings as well!

And to my brothers and sisters in Christ at New Hope OPC.
You bring out the beauty of our great expectation.

CONTENTS

Acknowledgments   7

Introduction: What's at Stake   11

Part 1: Why Can't Men and Women Be Friends?

1. We're Letting the Wrong Voices Tell Us Who We Are   21
2. We Don't View Each Other Holistically   33
3. We Don't Know Our Mission   49
4. We Misunderstand the Nature of Purity   63
5. We're Immature and Fearful   79
6. We've Forgotten What Friendship Really Is   95
7. We've Overlooked Our Biblical Status as Brothers and Sisters   111

Part 2: How Do We Live as Sacred Siblings?

8. Find Our Sibling Identity in Our Elder Brother   131
9. Cultivate a Church Environment That Supports Sacred Siblingship   145
10. Promote One Another's Holiness   167
11. Enjoy Table Fellowship Together   183
12. Celebrate and Suffer Together   199
13. Model Affectionate, Appropriate Relationships to the Watching World   213

Conclusion: What Now?   231

Appendix: Siblings in Scripture   235

ACKNOWLEDGMENTS

One event above all others spurred me to answer the notorious question about relationships between the sexes: "Why can't we be friends?" Four years ago, the Alliance of Confessing Evangelicals invited me to join Dr. Carl Trueman and Rev. Todd Pruitt in cohosting a podcast called *Mortification of Spin*. I was pleased to be able to contribute a laywoman's perspective alongside two godly pastors, one of whom was an accomplished academic as well. And I fit in easily as we bounced ideas off one another, engaged in theological conversation, and enjoyed a sibling-like banter that came naturally to us. But, to my surprise, some listeners soon warned of the dangers of having a woman interacting with two respectable men. Some of the "warnings" were terribly demeaning: I was an affair waiting to happen, a possible career ender, perhaps Satan's strategy to bring down another pastor and church. Even if I was a positive addition to the podcast, it wasn't worth the risk. The underlying message was that we shouldn't model this coed dynamic to the church. Even if our relationships and interactions were godly, coed friendship is not something everyone can handle. Don't try this at home.

We were all surprised. Had we done something wrong? All of a sudden, our sexuality was an elephant in the room. We had to address it with one another, with our spouses, and with our boss. I am glad that none of us believed the spin. I want to thank Catriona Trueman and Karen Pruitt for not looking at me in this reductive way. I want to thank the Alliance for risking the loss of donors in order to keep me on the program. And I want to thank Carl and Todd for all the razzing, humor, support, protectiveness, friendship—and did I mention razzing?—that I should expect from older spiritual brothers. Friendship isn't a profession; our coed dynamic on the podcast works so well because we are friends with one another in real life. And so this book is appropriately a mortification of spin.

I have wonderful friends. That's why the research for *Why Can't We Be Friends?* was particularly joyful work—the more I uncovered, the more my heart grew thankful for the people in my life. I particularly want to thank my parents for raising my siblings and me in an atmosphere that promoted brother and sister relationships of faith, love, honor, trust, healthy competition, humor, and solidarity. And I want to thank my church, New Hope OPC, which showcases a household full of loving siblings in Christ. Both the household I was raised in and the household of God that my family worships in testify to our Lord's great mercy in giving us a taste of what is to come. The beauty of our siblingship that we enjoy now is like the sparkling morning dew that refreshes the hope we share together for the new heavens and the new earth.

One particular brother in Christ has been pivotal in this project. So I want to especially thank my elder, Dave Myers, for all his encouragement and interest, for reading my chapters critically, and for the many great insights and questions that helped to improve the manuscript. The footnote credits to you that are peppered throughout the book make me smile; they testify in a practical way to God's gift of friendship between the sexes and to the fruit of the ministry in local churches.

Thanks are always in order to my husband, Matt, who continually models in action all the big ideas that I like to theologize about. You make it look so simple. Thank you for blessing me with twenty years of loving marriage. You are the type of husband and friend who gives great credibility to the words I write. You lay your life down for mine every day and still manage to be a loving friend to others. Our marriage blesses our friendships, and our friendships bless our marriage.

And many thanks to the P&R team for all they have put into this book. I appreciate the support from Ian Thompson and Amanda Martin, who encouraged me to write on this topic, as well as all the work poured into its fruition. And I always appreciate the work of Aaron Gottier in my final stages of editing.

INTRODUCTION

What's at Stake

This is a book that I didn't want to write—until I really wanted to write it. I couldn't *not* write it.

The strange thing is that I know this will be a controversial book. I'm going to make the case that men and women can and should be friends, along with describing a biblical theology that answers why and how we can pull this off. In fact, I will argue that Christian men and women are more than friends—we are brothers and sisters in Christ, and we need to act according to who (and whose) we are.

Already, after reading these few short lines, you may have formed a strong opinion of me. Maybe you think it's crazy to even have to write a book about something so obvious, or maybe you think I'm completely naive about how men and women think and what leads to affairs. That's why I didn't want to write this book.

My own view on this issue has changed throughout the twenty years of my marriage. In the past, I would never have flat-out stated that men and women can't be friends at all. I don't expect most of my readers think that either. But I had a big pile of caveats that made me wonder. Does friendship hurt marriage? Does marriage hinder friendships?

I see these questions in others as well. Most Christians who wonder if men and women can be friends are passionate about purity and faithfulness in our marriages. We want to be smart. We don't want to be naive about sin or to cause anyone to stumble. We want our marriages to last, affair and pornography free, and we want our sons and daughters to be chaste. We expect the church to be a safe place amidst a sex-obsessed culture. But we have watched high-profile, respected pastors become involved in devastating sexual scandal. We have seen friends fall into sexual sin. Some of us are children of divorce due to affairs. And some have been victims in our own marriages. Sexual sin is painfully destructive. When we think of the power of temptation and the ramifications of sexual sin, it seems natural to ask whether men and women can be friends. Many people caution that attempting friendship is just playing with fire. Why risk it?

Over my years of blogging and social media experience, I have discovered that some topics bring out the fighters on both sides. Sometimes I've been surprised at the divided responses to things I have written about—things like women's bathing suit choices, gluten, the Trinity, and who can teach Sunday school. Sure, I expect people to have strong convictions. But we also need to be discerning about which hills we are actually going to die on. Some topics, like the Trinity, are worth duking it out over—but I've decided that I don't want to provoke unneeded controversy on an issue such as gluten. It's just not worth losing friends over. I've learned to pick my battles.

Well, friendship between the sexes is another hot button that provokes passionate interaction. It's an issue that the church has often stubbed its toe on. And I'm just foolhardy enough to write a book about it! Why, Aimee; *why?*

Our Relationships

I wrote this book because I want us to be biblically faithful in a very important area: our relationships. I want marriages to be better. I want singles to have more meaningful relationships. And I want the next generation to grow up with a better understanding of how men and women view each other.

What is the quality of your relationships? How would you describe your relationships in the home? In the workplace? In the church? In the neighborhood? If you're single, how's that going for you? What about if you're dating? If you're married, how is your marriage? Do you tend to be jealous or suspicious? Scared? Guilty? Superior? Are you lonely? Unsatisfied? Maybe you're just stressed trying to live a life of purity and not really sure what that looks like from day to day. What do you do when you're attracted to someone? What happens when you suddenly have teenagers who are at dating age? Is that even a thing? If you're married and have to work closely with the other sex,[1] how hypervigilant do you need to be? Can you drive to a meeting or share a lunch break with a person of the other sex? If you're a pastor who wants to shepherd your whole congregation well, is your office off limits to half (or more) of your congregation? What about email? Can men and women email?

You see, a lot of questions fall underneath the broad

1. Thanks to Matt Vos, professor of sociology and chair of the sociology department at Covenant College, for pointing out to me that by using the language "opposite sex" we frame one another as opposites when in reality men and women are more alike than they are different, we predispose one another to push away the other sex, and we perpetuate the notion of "woman as other," which leads to abuses.

question of whether men and women can be friends. We assume that we know the meaning of friendship in that question, but I have discovered that many people do not.

In this book, I am going to argue that men and women in the church should not only be friends, but actually be more than friends. Unfortunately, as eager as the conservative church is to speak out against the sexual revolution and gender identity theories, she often appears just as reductive as the culture surrounding her when it comes to representing our communion with God in our communion with one another. But Scripture tells us over and over again that Christian men and women are more than friends—we are brothers and sisters in Christ. Paul tells Timothy to treat gender distinction in a familial way. He petitions him to appeal to the older men as fathers, "the younger men as brothers, the older women as mothers, and the younger women as sisters, in all purity" (1 Tim. 5:1–2). This says it all. Paul doesn't give Timothy a bunch of details on how to treat a father or a sister; we already know how to do that. It's a respectful way to relate to one another—and, when we relate this way, we remove the possibility of sex.

We have lost the beauty of brotherhood and sisterhood— distinction between the sexes that doesn't reduce them to sex alone. The way that we relate to one another sends a message—to one another and to the watching world—about who we are. We are God's people! And in his Word, we can learn a lot about the types of relationships he wants us to have in his household.

When we start talking about whether a man and a woman can be friends, we begin to question God's plan for human sexuality. Is our sexuality to be ultimately expressed in the union of one man and one woman in marriage? Is sex the fundamental expression of our sexuality? Will we be sexual beings in the new heavens and the new earth? If so, how will we express our sexuality in eternity, and how does that affect the way we relate to one another now?

Our Theology

These questions can't be hashed out 140 characters at a time on social media threads. They can't be answered well in a series of blog posts or on a conversational podcast. And I am convinced that there's too much at stake—both theologically and practically—for me to keep watching them be argued in magazine articles and Twitter threads. I can't take it anymore. I want to address what's behind the "Why can't we be friends?" question. And I want to do it in a reasonable tone so that those on both sides of the issue can come together and engage with me. We have the same concerns, and we all need to be sharpened.

Many of the current prescriptions for appropriate behavior for men and women have skipped over the foundational thinking that helps us to grow in wisdom, discernment, and fruitful relationships. Four theological categories underlie the answer to this friendship question, and I'll need to use some theological terms for the sake of precision. Throughout this book, we will see that what we believe in these four areas affects how we view relationships between the sexes:

- *Anthropology—the study of human beings.* Why were we created? Why does that matter? A theological anthropology is the foundation to our understanding of friendship. We are created for communion with God and one another.
- *Christology—the study of Christ.* Who are we as Christians? We can't discuss this without talking about Jesus Christ and what he has done on our behalf. Our union with

15

Christ, our Elder Brother, gives God's people a new relationship as brothers and sisters.

- *Ecclesiology—the study of the church.* When we talk about God's church and the men and women in it, we talk about God's *household* (see 1 Tim. 3:15). We are God's family. How does he expect us to treat one another?
- *Eschatology—the study of the end times and eternity.* How does the whole Christian life end? What is our ultimate hope, and how does it shape our relationships? What we expect in the future should shape our behavior here and now.

We will study these ideas as we work through the practical aspects of improving our lives together, aiming toward holy, joyful living that glorifies God.

Our Sibling Status

Some passages of Scripture directly address men or women, but numerous passages in the New Testament are directed to the entire church. In these cases, the biblical writers use the familial term *adelphoi,* meaning "brothers and sisters." This description appears many times. However, most Scripture translations use the word *brethren* or *brothers* instead. As we navigate the distinctions between men and women in an overly sexualized world, it's important for us to be aware of when the New Testament writers were including both brothers *and* sisters in their audience. It is extremely helpful in the discussion of masculinity and femininity and how we relate. The Christian Standard Bible uses *brothers and sisters,* and it really makes a difference when you are reading through a book like 1 Thessalonians and find yourself underlining twenty instances of this language!

What I can't find in Scripture is any warning about avoiding friendship between the sexes in order to avoid sin. Instead the Bible says, "Let love be without hypocrisy. Detest evil; cling to what is good" (Rom. 12:9 csb). We are to *cling* to what is good, not throw it out because sin is possible. Directly following that command is a call to meaningful relationships with our siblings in Christ: "Love one another deeply as brothers and sisters" (Rom. 12:10 csb).

I grew up with a brother and a sister, and I was blessed with additional twin brothers when I was twenty-four years old. We have different mothers, but I shudder to call them half-brothers. They are my brothers, and I have the same affection for them as for the brother I grew up with. My family has always valued the blessing of siblingship. When I first began to notice sibling language all over Scripture, it resonated with me. I already know how to love brothers and sisters deeply, because this is something I already do. So it was especially exciting for me to research siblingship in antiquity and how the original readers of Scripture would have connected with that language as well.

The shocking part was how little I could find written on this topic. Christians are continually addressed as brothers and sisters in the New Testament, but there are only a few obscure books on Christian friendships between the sexes and even fewer on the scriptural language of siblingship. You will notice that I have gone outside my usual base for research. The topic of holy friendship is broader than Protestantism, and I have found richness in the contributions of Christians from different traditions who have thought deeply on this topic. And thank goodness for rare dissertations (though not for the cost of buying published ones) for providing academic work on a topic that accomplished authors don't want to touch! Why are so few Christian academics, pastors, and authors writing about this?

Faithful Friendship

As we look at the big, controversial question of this book's title, we will answer some other questions:

- Are we being faithful to Scripture when we talk about and live out our relationships between the sexes?
- What responsibilities do we have before God and to one another?
- How should the church model richness in relationships before the watching world?

In part 1, we'll look at the reasons why friendship between the sexes is so difficult—why we can't seem to be friends. Part 2 shifts to what friends do. Every chapter aims to build my case that there is no need for friendship between the sexes to be a controversial topic. Instead it should be one that glorifies our truest friend and Elder Brother, Jesus Christ.

PART 1

Why Can't Men and Women Be Friends?

1

We're Letting the Wrong
Voices Tell Us Who We Are

We can say a lot *about* ourselves, but how often do we think about who we *are*?

Who am I? As easy as this question sounds to answer, especially for a Christian, we may be surprised to hear some of the responses that those who know us in different contexts would give about us. How would our friends answer this question? Does who we are make a difference in our relationships? How well do our acquaintances and friends really know us? How much of that "knowledge" is merely an image that we *want* them to believe? Are they buying it? What messages have we absorbed from others, and do those messages affect what we communicate about ourselves?

Who are you when safely protected within the walls of your home? Who are you when you walk through the doors of your local church? Who are you to your neighbors and coworkers? Who are you to your extended family? Who are you in the presence of your friends? While integrity calls us to be the same person no matter where we are and whom we are talking to, we don't always have that freedom.

Mixed Messages

In my childhood, I learned a lot about my identity in relation to my family. In particular, I learned a lot about gender relations by being a sister. My interactions with my sister and brother, and the way our parents treated us, prepared me well for friendship and marriage, living and relating with those outside our household, and one day creating a household of my own. And to this day, my sister and I take credit for how our brother turned out to be such a great friend to others and also a wonderful husband to his wife. As the middle sibling sandwiched between two sisters, my brother Luke learned all about the beautiful, the mysterious, and the ugly of femininity. The three of us learned that we were indispensible members of our household and that we were to build one another up, especially in public. We were equally challenged to live active lives physically, academically, and spiritually.

My siblings know me well. They know my strengths and weaknesses, my way of thinking, my sense of humor, my fears, and my longings. We grew up having fun together, and we also learned to suffer together. We have history. I never felt hindered by my gender[1] in my personal household. I felt equipped and responsible.

---

1. Here's as good a place as any to point out that many today suggest that gender is merely a social construct. Should I even use that word? Our *sex* has to do with our biology. The differences between the male and female sexes include, but are not limited to, our chromosomes, our muscle mass, our genitalia, our hormones, and even the way we process information. But that's not really what I'm referring to here. *Gender* describes how the two sexes relate to each other socially. Gender often carries the cultural baggage of a society. But gender is also real—when we talk about how we relate, we talk about gender, socially constructed or not.

Who am I? I'm a sister and a daughter. I'm blessed.

But, as I was growing up, the culture around me sent messages suggesting that I needed to look a certain way and make myself desirable and available. The world told me that I am autonomous and should use my sexuality to please myself and get what I want.

The year I entered high school, the popular movie *When Harry Met Sally* released, and Harry Burns, played by Billy Crystal, told the world that "men and women can't be friends because the sex part always gets in the way."[2] One movie helped to popularize the notion that all women are reduced to a means of sexual gratification for men, that a man cannot control himself from thinking about conquering every woman he is "friends" with, and that we all have to live with this cold, hard fact. It was in the movies, so it must be true.

Who am I? I'm a woman who is to use her best assets to attract and manipulate a man. I am empowered by choice for my own body and ambitions.

The church, God's household, ought to speak to us about our truest identity through the ministry of the Word. Even the outside culture expects the church to respond with a higher calling than the world offers. But over time I learned that much of the conservative church believes the "Billy Crystal rule" taught by Burns. In a complete contradiction of our fight to uphold a biblical understanding of sexuality, Hollywood became our teacher on relationships and gender after all. The church sent messages that a woman's attractiveness serves the purpose of landing a husband, then becomes a threat to all other men. My sexuality became a barrier to friendship. This has been quite a challenge in my adult years.

---

2. "Men and Women," *When Harry Met Sally...*, directed by Rob Reiner, written by Nora Ephron (1989; Los Angeles: MGM, 2015), DVD.

Who am I? I am a woman, created to find a husband and fashion a haven for him. And I am a threat to other people's marriages.

As you can see, my personal household, the outside world, and the church have given me conflicting messages about who I am and why that matters.

In Search of Mature Sexuality and Relationships

I married at the young age of twenty-one with immature views on sexuality. In hindsight, it's as if I moved backward from the healthy understanding of gender and relationships I had learned in my family growing up. I had adopted worldly views about men and women from both the secular culture and the church at large. I wanted to be a good wife. I wanted to do the whole biblical womanhood thing. I pursued it with vigor. Encouraged by a popular Christian radio program, my husband and I came up with rules that would protect our marriage from affairs. But I also looked to my husband to fulfill more of my relational needs than he possibly could. I thought that our marriage and growing family would supply all our needs for companionship.

To make things more complicated, my husband worked with a lot of women. As the owner of a coffee café, I was also meeting a lot of people. Coffee baristas function like bartenders. We have regulars and learn much more about them than how they like their coffee. And while the little church plant that we joined had a great community in which men and women interacted well together, I quickly received signals from my pastor that women don't learn theology at the same level as men. This glass ceiling of expectation for women learning theology and communicating it with other brothers and sisters in the faith was a lonely reality for me.

My husband and I have been married for over twenty years now. In this time, we have grown and learned a lot about relationships. We have come up against some strange views in the church about manhood and womanhood. On one hand, we see regular laypeople with fruitful coed friendships. On the other, we have been taught that this is dangerous territory.

I'd love to be able to point the secular culture to Christ's church as a representation of how communion with God affects relationships between the sexes. But we've reduced a lot of the discussion about manhood in the church to how a man shows authority. Much of the discussion about womanhood draws lines nitpicking what a woman can do and what she can't do. And the church has provided little discussion about how men and women relate to each other.

Worse, I have come across some troubling remarks in the broader evangelical subculture about Christian stewardship to our neighbors, friendship between the sexes, and the value of a woman's contribution. I've read my share of articles about whether a man and a woman can text, share a car ride, or eat a business lunch together in a public place. I even read an argument from a popular pastor considering whether it's okay for a man who is lost to ask a housewife for directions without this challenging his manhood.[3] I've seen high-profile pastors write and share disturbing tweets such as this one: "I could see giving a woman a ride. To the hospital. If the bone was sticking out."[4]

This kind of talk makes my heart sink on so many levels. *Who am I?* I'm such a threat to a man's faithfulness and

---

3. See John Piper, "A Vision of Biblical Complementarity," in *Recovering Biblical Manhood and Womanhood: A Response to Evangelical Feminism*, ed. John Piper and Wayne Grudem (1991; repr., Wheaton, IL: Crossway, 2006), 50.

4. Douglas Wilson, (@douglaswils), "Pence Rule: Case by Case Dept.," Twitter, April 6, 2017, 4:20 p.m., https://twitter.com/douglaswils/status/85012615554 6062848.

a pastor's reputation that I'm barely worth the risk of a ride to the hospital. Thirty years after *When Harry Met Sally*, some pastors have taken Harry Burns's pronouncement to a whole new level.

I wish I could say that I'm just pointing out a few extremes, but I've received this message over and over again in my own life. I see godly men who want to interact with women with a clear conscience but who are brainwashed by the Billy Crystal rule. Some of the very men who preach biblical manhood and chivalry do nothing when it will actually cost them something—and that cost is usually "appearances." This really hit home when I once found myself in a strange city, at night, in the rain, walking down a sketchy alley when I could have been offered a ride to my car three blocks away. In those situations, I cringe to answer the question *Who am I?*

The Damaging Consequences of Our Message

Men and women can't be friends until we stop letting the wrong voices tell us who we are. Our identity matters. If we listen to conflicting voices that tell us we are adversaries, consumerists, or dangerous to the other sex, then we are in no position to be friends because we will accept the false labels and behave accordingly. In effect, we will live a lie!

Hollywood promotes sex without consequences, and people believe it. When women are displayed as seductresses and men as consumers, it's not surprising when some men think they are entitled to gratify all their desires. Women pay the price as more powerful men abuse and devalue them.

The disastrous effects of this thinking have begun to boil to the surface. In the fall of 2017, after close to one hundred women came forward to accuse powerful film producer and Hollywood executive Harvey Weinstein of sexual harassment, assault, and rape, actress Alyssa Milano called women to share their own stories: "If all the women who have been sexually harassed or assaulted wrote 'Me too' as a status, we might give people a sense of the magnitude of the problem."[5] In response, millions of people engaged in the #MeToo discussion on social media. It was devastating to read story after story from these suffering women. It was also empowering for women to feel like they had a voice—and that their voice mattered.

But the story didn't end there. Shortly afterward, the #ChurchToo hashtag appeared, as women testified of sexual abuse by those in the church.[6] As if the violation to their bodies weren't dehumanizing enough, woman after woman shared horrifying reactions from church leaders who did not believe them, shamed them, or told them they needed to repent for provoking the act. These women had no voice in the church, and the voices that they heard did not advocate for them. The silence of their supposed friends and the voices of those leaders who let them down told women that they weren't valued as sisters in Christ, that they weren't created with inherent dignity, and that their contributions weren't welcome.

Is the church, like Hollywood, perpetuating an environment in which she is vulnerable to or complicit in abuse? In the aftermath, will we label all men and women and be led by fear, or will we look to God's Word to see how he calls us to relate? It's easy for us to look at Hollywood and say, "I told you so." The message they promote about sex is now reaping the consequences. But what do the consequences we are seeing in

---

5. Quoted in Nadia Khomami, "#MeToo: how a hashtag became a rallying cry against sexual harassment," *The Guardian*, October 20, 2017, https://www .theguardian.com/world/2017/oct/20/women-worldwide-use-hashtag-metoo -against-sexual-harassment.

6. See Casey Quackenbush, "The Religious Community Is Speaking Out Against Sexual Violence With #ChurchToo," *TIME*, November 22, 2017, http://time .com/5034546/me-too-church-too-sexual-abuse/.

the #ChurchToo response reveal about the church's message? What does the church teach about men, women, what we are created for, and how we are to relate to each other?

Anthropology and the Sexes

When discussing relationships between men and women, we don't want our personal households, the culture at large, or the household of God to espouse reductive views of the sexes. All three can answer the question *Who am I?* in different, often troubling, ways. And, as we've seen, the consequences can be dire for both individuals and groups. Which message is true?

In his excellent essay on theological anthropology, Kelly Kapic answers many of the problems proposed in the first chapters of this book.[7] A proper theological anthropology gets to the heart of who we truly are. What does it mean for human beings to be put on this earth together as men and women? We find the answer revealed in God's Word, and Kapic has done some heavy lifting academically from which we can build fruitful applications.

Kapic explains that we must "[look] to the incarnate Christ" to "discover the Triune Creator, the human creature, and the particular call and response that hold [them] together."[8] By looking to Christ in order to understand the relationship between God and his image bearers, we can develop a theological anthropology that "faithfully reflects God's purposes as well as the reality of current human existence—including dignity and struggle, universality and particularity, relationality

---

7. See Kelly M. Kapic, "Anthropology," chap. 8 in *Christian Dogmatics: Reformed Theology for the Church Catholic*, ed. Michael Allen and Scott R. Swain (Grand Rapids: Baker Academic, 2016).

8. Kapic, 166.

and personal identity, all understood within the framework of love and communion."[9]

The "Triune Creator" calls us into communion with himself. This simply stated sentence is full of wonder! *Communion* is an intimate participation in fellowship. It "is mutual trust, mutual belonging; it is the to-and-fro movement of love between two people where each gives and each one receives."[10] God has created us to share in the Father's love for the Son, by his Holy Spirit.

We know about the blessed communion between the persons of the Trinity, but how are we included in that as mere creatures? In the incarnation, God affirms both creation and humanity. God isn't stingy with his love for the Son but is outgoing, generously calling us to share and participate in that love with him. "In Jesus, God actualizes his call to us to enter communion with him through the Son and by the Spirit."[11]

This is how Kapic frames his Christian anthropology. It is not merely philosophical but is rooted in the incarnate Christ. So, in the act of the incarnation, we see that the Father's love for humanity is preeminent in Christ, the one to whose likeness we are being transformed in our sanctification. This means everything when we are talking about who we are: those created in the image of God. We get to be like God! How do we do that, you ask? Kapic echoes John Owen in affirming that *"we are never more like God than when we love his Son through his Spirit."*[12]

The way we treat others in the church and in our vocations sends a message about their Creator. For example, as a

9. Kapic, 166.
10. Kapic, 178, quoting Jean Vanier, *Becoming Human* (Mahwah, NJ: Paulist Press, 2008), 28.
11. Kapic, "Anthropology," 167.
12. Kapic, 166.

public school teacher and administrator, my husband not only works with a lot of women but is a friend to many of them. He respects them, learns from them, and enjoys their presence (well, some of them, anyway), and he also protects them and helps them to flourish. These women know that he is safe. More than that, they can trust him to act as a friend who sees their value, worth, and contributions.

Unlike Harry Burns, and society at large, Matt doesn't hold a self-serving outlook on humanity in which men are consumers. Nor does he avoid women out of fear. Matt's theology accounts for platonic relational development, sacrificial giving, and accountability to a higher being. The way he treats the women at his work honors God, and it honors me as his wife. Despite the many voices in the evangelical subculture that have told us differently, we've come to learn that our godly friendships outside our marriage are not a threat but actually benefit the unique, exclusive communion that we have as husband and wife.

God's Word upholds the dignity of the sexes, the beautiful complexity in our design, and the way we are to relate to one another. How many people has God created so far? I can't even fathom the answer to that question. How many people does God add to his covenant family in a day? Only God knows. But those of us who are like him in loving his Son through his Spirit are also going to be like him in being outgoing with that love. It is a love that overflows into communion with one another.

The question *Who am I?* directly affects our relationships with both men and women. When we listen to the wrong voices, we either become afraid of each other or try to take advantage of or manipulate one another. This is not the way that God has called us to relate. In a time of sexual chaos, we see over-sexualization of men and women, sexual abuse and perversion, calls for gender fluidity and androgyny, and even the promotion of transgendered lifestyles. It is imperative for the church to speak God's Word to us about who we are.

I don't want to pretend to be androgynous. It's impossible, really. I am always aware that I am a woman. I am aware of this when I talk to other women and little girls, and when I talk to men and little boys. This awareness doesn't merely have to do with my physical body. It's part of the essence of who I am. When I communicate, I express myself as both a woman and a fellow human being. But more than that, I have been adopted into a holy household as a child of God, and my identity as a sister in that household shapes my communion with others. It shapes the way I relate to both fellow Christians and unbelievers as well.

It's important for us to examine whether our confessional theology (what we say we believe) and our functional theology (our operating beliefs in real life) are congruent. When we do this, we begin to see why it matters so much to learn theology. A good theological anthropology will tell us why a proper identity matters. Developing a rich understanding of our origin and purpose reveals what matters to God and, therefore, what should matter to us. First we will look at how our theology here affects whether we view one another in reductive or holistic ways. This is imperative to answering the question, why can't we be friends?

Discussion Questions

1. Who were some influential voices from home, church, and society that affected your perception of who you are? What messages did they send?
2. How might we discover a rich answer to who we are by looking to the incarnate Christ? Within the framework

of love and communion in Christ, what can we learn about dignity and struggle, universality and particularity, and relationality and personal identity?

3. Write a statement answering these questions: Who are you, and what is your purpose? How does this affect the way you relate to both men and women?

2

We Don't View Each
Other Holistically

Friendship between men and women is a taboo topic in the evangelical subculture. It makes us uncomfortable. Apparently, we are all time bombs on the brink of having an affair—or of being accused of having one. Because of this, men and women often feel uncomfortable around each other, even in innocent contexts, and we impose strict hedges on behavior in order to avoid the threat of sexual impropriety.

Most of us instinctively know what constitutes sexual impropriety in conversation and action—but, due to influence from our overly sexualized culture, we tend to scandalize ordinary acts of kindness and business. It becomes suspect to give someone a ride, share a meal with a coworker in a public place, or text the other sex without copying our spouses or another third party. Prohibitions of these acts are couched in language of protecting our purity, honoring our spouses, or wisely avoiding the threat of temptation. Challenge any of these suggestions, however, and the language of danger is invoked. If these ordinary acts are dangerous, it must be down-right foolish to use a meaningful term like *friendship* to describe a relationship between the sexes.

Do ordinary acts of kindness and business give you anxiety? Have you been reluctant to introduce someone of the other sex as your friend? Even in something as simple as a conversation with someone of the other sex, there seem to be too many ambiguous factors. *Am I holding eye contact too long? Oh no, I just laughed at his joke—is someone going to think I'm flirting? Is my body language sending the wrong signals?* These can be noble questions in certain situations. However, if we view one another more holistically, they don't have to be a common anxiety.

Distinction without Reduction

There are plenty of distinctions between men and women, and cross-sex friendships are different from same-sex ones. Let's not pretend that this isn't true! But distinctions are special qualities, and we should never be reductive about them. When we reduce others because of their physical assets or on the basis of ideas we've received from cultural expectations, we fall into objectifying or stereotyping men and women who are made in the image of God.

A healthy dynamic between men and women engages the whole person. In my family, I was raised with a proper understanding of distinction between the sexes without reduction. Having a brother helped me to understand an aspect of my own sisterhood and femininity that was distinct from what I learned about my sisterhood and femininity in my relationship with my sister. In all my family relationships, I had a sense that my mind, body, and soul were valued, and I thrived.

Society's message, however, is for both sexes to follow our baser instincts. *When Harry Met Sally* is the cultural icon of this mind-set—Harry representing every man, and Sally every woman. Sex is the endgame of all Harry's friendships with women: he pursues friendship in order to get sex, or he dismisses women whom he isn't interested in sexually pursuing, which is equally demeaning.[1] When Harry tells Sally that men and women can't be friends because the "sex part always gets in the way," we Sallies read between the lines. Our holistic personhood is not valued—friendship is merely a conduit to sex. Man's baser instinct overshadows anything else that matters. Savvy Sallies may as well accept the facts and maximize on this outlook by using their sexual appeal to get what they want. Reduced to objects of physical pleasure and consumption, women become a commodity.

Harry Burns isn't the only one to blame. Decades before *When Harry Met Sally* came out, Sigmund Freud reduced all affection to erotic desire—to our genitals—meaning that every look, gesture, touch, and thought holds sexual motives. That sounds jarring and crude, but it is in our history, so we need to talk about it. Freud's psychology still affects the thinking of our postmodern age. His explanation of maturity revolves around which psychosexual stage we've reached in life. These are genitally oriented stages showcasing a male superiority, in which females go through an anxious stage of penis envy before reaching mature sexual identity. This view reduces friendship, whether it is same-sex or cross-sex, to role-playing for sexual gratification.

The church has accepted and semi-sanctified these reductive views: sexuality is good for landing a spouse, but it's a barrier to friendship because men and women can't possibly just enjoy each other's company. We associate all intimacy with the bedroom, so we expect every meaningful interaction between a man and a woman to be laden with repressed sexual

1. Thanks to my elder, Dave Myers, for this point.

desire. That means that all intellectual, creative, entertaining, or conversational enjoyment with someone of the other sex needs to be fulfilled by our spouses. That's an awfully heavy load for one person to bear!

Harry Burns isn't interested in friendship with women because he can't look at them as friends. The wider evangelical mind-set doesn't quite put it that way. Acts of friendship are viewed as "unnecessary temptation." (What falls under the purview of *necessary* temptation, one wonders.) As one person responded to me, saying and doing are two different things. Saying that we should resist our sinful, base instincts and pursue pure friendships no matter the gender is a "'good preaching but hard living' bit of church-talk that isn't especially helpful."[2] Sure, we're told, friendship is biblical and sounds good, but it isn't necessary and isn't worth the trouble of fighting the sin in my own heart. Your body is a threat to me, and I must protect myself from you.

Of course, this is pitched as an act of protection for both parties. Men and women are reduced to a temptation and a danger to each other. Acts of friendship are all suspect; therefore it feels much safer for us all to keep them taboo.

But if friendship doesn't matter, then a lot of other parts of our design don't matter either.

"The Whole Person Matters"[3]

The design of creation reveals a lot to us. God didn't create anything that doesn't matter. So all our faculties that reflect

2. Rob Hawkins, November 2017, comment on Aimee Byrd, "Pickpocketing Purity," *Housewife Theologian* (blog), *Mortification of Spin*, November 16, 2017, http://www.mortificationofspin.org/mos/housewife-theologian/pickpocketing -purity#.Wh7VybT82uU.

3. Kelly M. Kapic, "Anthropology," from *Christian Dogmatics: Reformed Theology*

the image of God—our minds, bodies, wills, emotions, and souls—need to be rightly ordered toward God in communion with him, because they all matter.

What does that look like? Before the fall, man and woman had minds that knew God truly, if not exhaustively. They had a holy emotional and spiritual life, with righteous hearts, a will to please God, and the desire to do so. Their affections, thoughts, and actions—the whole person—glorified God. This is rightly ordered goodness and purity.[4] After the fall, the situation changed; but those redeemed by God know that the original, holistic design revealed in creation will be restored to us when we are glorified in the new heavens and the new earth. Our design will be perfected to its proper end in Christ.

As Kelly Kapic suggested in chapter 1, this points us to the incarnation. The Son took on flesh, and that shows us that our bodies are important. They matter. All our human faculties needed to be redeemed: mind, body, and soul. When Jesus took on true human nature, he lived a holistic life of faith and obedience. His mind, affections, and desires were rightly ordered in holiness. As Christians are transformed into the likeness of the Son, we look forward to intimate communion with him, in new resurrected bodies, in the new heavens and the new earth.

It's hard to think of a future when our minds will be free from sinful thoughts, our hearts will long only for righteousness, and our bodies will serve God with perfect stewardship. It sounds too good to be true. But it is true! And the truth about our design and our glorification should profoundly affect us in the present. Kapic writes, "The Scriptures do not belittle human physicality but instead assume the body is a gift from God. And for our purposes, our bodies were meant to foster

---

for the Church Catholic, ed. Michael Allen and Scott R. Swain (Grand Rapids: Baker Academic, 2016), 170.

4. See Kapic, 172.

communion and love rather than undermine them."[5] Our sexuality matters. Men and women together bear the image of God in humanity. That means we need to view our sisters and brothers holistically, not just physically. When we look at people as holistic, relational beings, we don't reduce them to their bodies—specifically to their genitalia and sexual urges. Our femininity and masculinity are more than that.

It also means our physicality should not pose a threat to one another. Is our zealousness to avoid sin inadvertently training Christians to reduce women to sexual temptresses and men to animalistic impulses? We are to be transformed by the renewing of our minds (see Rom. 12:2). To view the other sex as constant temptations to sin and threats to purity merely perpetuates the thinking and behavior of the unredeemed.[6]

A Functional Family

A proper view of men and women leads to sanctification of the believer, glorifies our Creator and Savior, and promotes his worship. When we look at one another as holistic, relational beings, we don't reduce femininity and masculinity to cultural roles and stereotypes. Yet even the church can fall prey to that kind of thinking.

We often use the term *dysfunctional family* in a humorous, self-deprecating style to acknowledge that we don't have everything together in our personal households. The official definition of this term first appeared in a 1974 book published by a founder of the family therapy movement, Salvador Minuchin: "A dysfunctional family is a system that has responded to these

5. Kapic, 175.
6. In all this, I don't want to downplay the very real dangers of sexual sin. As a child of divorce, I value faithfulness in marriage in a way that I think some do not, who have not experienced the pain that separation and divorce causes.

internal or external demands for change by stereotyping its functioning."[7] In other words, a dysfunctional family defines the functions of each member in such a rigid way that no adjustment is made to allow for growth.

Minuchin's analysis requires some qualifications. Some important parameters do not change; the household needs them to function under good order. There is no function in chaos. Husbands don't become wives, sisters don't become brothers, and parents don't become children. We change and grow with the goal of being sanctified within the responsibilities and relationships we have to one another, not of escaping them. But our responsibilities and relationships change as we grow and meet different circumstances. For example, parents are to equip their children to become adults who are independent of them. Both controlling and enabling parents are dysfunctional. Yet as a child becomes an adult and builds a household of her own, her parents still function as parents, only in a new capacity. The things that do not change are anchors for function and growth.

Still, Minuchin is correct that stereotyping blocks growth and leads to dysfunction. In God's household, the church, certain unchanging qualifications for ministry are put in place (see 1 Tim. 3:1–13; Titus 1:5–9). But beyond that, men and women are often assigned roles that align with conventional beliefs and hinder their ability to grow. Women are stereotyped as sentimental damsels who need not worry about theology. Men are stereotyped as power-obsessed rationalists who can never empathize or nurture. These are extreme views, though I have seen them more times than I care to count.

Even when we don't hold to such extreme versions of these stereotypes, they still influence the way we try to function,

---

7. Salvador Minuchin, *Families and Family Therapy* (Cambridge, MA: Harvard University Press, 1974), 110.

leading us to create women's ministries and men's ministries that many feel alienated from. Not all men want to camp and white-water raft while drinking craft beer and discussing supra-lapsarianism. And not all women want to learn how to make centerpieces at the annual spring tea while listening to a light message on a pink passage of Scripture. These stereotypes are not implemented maliciously but are usually intended to serve the congregation well. Still, they contribute to dysfunction in God's household.

Stereotypes can be even subtler. Men are often encouraged and equipped with leadership skills, while women are left unsharpened. Masculinity's machismo portrayal in much Christian literature leaves men who are less physical and aggressive feeling like they are less of a man. Single women in the church are expected to participate in studies that focus mainly on the specified roles of a wife and mother. Some women have pointed out that what is portrayed as "biblical womanhood" often describes your typical white woman in upper-middle-class society.[8] Is this really how Scripture portrays godly manhood and womanhood?

Stereotypes Overturned

In the few passages that address the specific responsibilities of men and women in relationship with each other, Scripture turns stereotypes upside down. One example is Ephesians 5:22–33. Many affirm that Paul calls men to sacrificial leadership in this text, but they usually place emphasis on the wife's call to submit to her husband. Teachers on

8. See, for example, Persis Lorenti, "The Face in the Reflection," *Tried with Fire* (blog), June 8, 2018, https://triedbyfire.blogspot.com/2017/06/the-face-in-reflection.html, and Jasmine Holmes, "That Time I Tweeted about Biblical Womanhood," *Not a Mommy Blog*, July 30, 2017, https://jasminelholmes.com/that-time-i-tweeted-about-biblical-womanhood/.

this passage urge husbands to be Christlike and wives to submit to their authority; then they present authority and submission as the lens for biblical manhood and womanhood.

But let's look at what Paul says in Ephesians 5:25–27:

> Husbands, love your wives, just as Christ also loved the church and gave Himself up for her, so that He might sanctify her, having cleansed her by the washing of water with the word, that He might present to Himself the church in all her glory, having no spot or wrinkle or any such thing; but that she would be holy and blameless.

New Testament professor Cynthia Westfall examines this passage in the context of gender roles in the Greco-Roman world, when women's low-status domestic work was comparable to slaves' work. This is what is so fascinating about what Paul says. Instead of addressing husbands according to their authority in the public domain as warriors, patrons, and providers, Paul uses imagery that features "household scenes of bathing, clothing (spinning and weaving), laundering, feeding, and nurturing, because Jesus is depicted as providing these services for the church, which is both his bride and his body."[9]

The actions that Paul describes for the men were considered "women's work," and the church that they are a part of is portrayed as a woman, a bride. Westfall writes that Paul "promotes a model of servanthood and low status, consistent with the humility of Christ's incarnation, precisely for men, who have power and position in the Greco-Roman social system."[10] Hearing this stereotypical women's work applied to men must have really grabbed the original audience's attention.

9. Cynthia Long Westfall, *Paul and Gender: Reclaiming the Apostle's Vision for Men and Women in Christ* (Grand Rapids: Baker Academic, 2016), 56.
10. Westfall, 23.

And reapplying these stereotypes carries important teaching that gets me excited! For example, what exactly does it mean for the church to be washed and presented "in all her glory" (v. 27)? Westfall suggests this language refers to a "bride's prenuptial washing, and the clothing and laundering (including spot removal, washing, and ironing) in 5:27 may refer to obtaining and maintaining a bride's wedding clothes."[11] She extends the reference of Christ sanctifying his church to have multiple meanings. At first we think of the eschatological presentation of Christ's bride, the church, without spot or wrinkle on that Great Day of his return for her. But this language causes us to look back, as well, all the way to Ezekiel 16:1–13, where this metaphor depicts God's covenant with Israel.

> At birth and at puberty, neither a midwife nor a mother nor a servant had love, pity, or compassion to care for the newborn Israel or to cleanse and clothe Israel when she reached puberty, so Yahweh performed these services for her.
>
> The force of the metaphor must not be lost or confused: both the Old Testament imagery and Paul are portraying God, Christ, and the husband as performing [domestic] services for a bride or wife.[12]

As he explains the responsibilities of headship in a household, Paul tells the men to serve in ways that were associated only with women's roles. Not only are female metaphors applied to the man here to teach how he is to love his wife, but also, as part of the church, men are called Christ's bride, adorned in feminine wedding garments.

11. Westfall, 57.
12. Westfall, 57.

Paul didn't invert stereotypes just once or twice. He calls both men and women to seek strength in the Lord (see Eph. 3:16; 6:10; Phil. 4:13; Col. 1:11; as well as Isa. 40:29, 31; Mark 12:30).[13] He calls both men and women to fight spiritual warfare as warriors (see Rom. 13:12; Eph. 6:10–17; 1 Thess. 5:8).[14] In Paul's day, only men were Olympic athletes, yet Paul exhorts both men and women to fight like boxers and run like Olympians in persevering to their goal of glorification with Christ (see 1 Cor. 9:24–27). Paul uses the language of soldiers in combat to encourage men and women to strive together for their heavenly citizenship (see Phil. 1:27–30). He describes Euodia and Syntyche as women who have "labored" (ESV), "contended" (CSB), or "struggle[d]" (NASB) with him in the gospel (see Phil. 4:2–3).[15] I am thankful that Paul didn't write separate epistles to the men and the women. It makes you wonder why we have separate women's Bibles now, doesn't it?

What may have been even more shocking to original readers of Scripture were the feminine metaphors of pregnancy, childbirth, and nursing mothers that Paul uses to describe his own leadership in the churches (see 1 Cor. 3:1–2; Gal. 4:19; 1 Thess. 2:6–7).[16] The Greco-Roman culture of the time promoted machismo masculine stereotypes that would never allow a man to proudly describe himself using any feminine traits.[17] Why would Paul risk his own manly qualifications for leadership with such provocative language?

Paul didn't describe androgynous function and relationships between men and women, but he smashed down unnecessary cultural stereotypes, using those very stereotypes to

---

13. For more on masculine and feminine metaphors applied to all believers, see Westfall, 46–56, which also provides these Scripture references.

14. See Westfall, 46–56.

15. See Westfall, 48.

16. See Westfall, 53.

17. See Westfall, 52–53.

redefine the responsibilities that men and women have in Christ's kingdom.

Let's Continue to Challenge Reductive Stereotyping

There was a time when women were considered incapable of virtue—meaning that the entire sex was unworthy of true friendship. Cicero, Aristotle, and Plato all wrote treatises on the virtue of friendship, which taught that women lacked the capacity to participate in this high form of communion. How could such renowned philosophers stereotype women in the most reductive way? They believed that it was not in a woman's nature to attain this kind of relational moral perfection in friendship. Even Augustine, "although he knew that well-educated and cultured women existed,"[18] and respected his own mother's wisdom, wrote, "If God had wanted Adam to have a partner in scintillating conversation he would have created another man."[19]

Few people, if any, think that women lack relational virtue anymore, yet we can still be reductive in placing fixed, dysfunctional roles on men and women. When we do, we overlook how Scripture turns stereotypes upside down by using the very language of the culture to arm both sexes as disciples of Christ.

Women should be invested in just as much as the men. Are the men and women in your church constantly in separate ministries? While it's good to build sister or brother relationships separately by gender sometimes, are there ample occasions for the men and women to serve and sharpen each other,

18. From Henry Chadwick's introduction to Saint Augustine, *Confessions*, trans. Henry Chadwick (Oxford: Oxford University Press, 1991), xviii.
19. St. Augustine, *Literal Commentary on Genesis*, quoted in ibid.

thereby growing together as a church? Are all laypeople given equal opportunities to serve in all capacities available to them? Or are the women expected to fill the childcare and kitchen spots, while the men are given more intellectually stimulating positions? These are good questions for a church to evaluate so that God's household can thrive.

Here is the thing. On the whole, men are created physically stronger than women, which does call them to responsibility in certain acts of soldiery, protection, and bravery. Women are created with the ability to support life in their wombs and strengthen babies with their own breasts, which does impose physical vulnerability and calls them to a responsibility to nurture and care. But that does not mean that women are without strength and that men are without vulnerability. It doesn't mean that women aren't called to bravery and protection or that men aren't called to nurture and care. None of us are to rely on our own abilities in God's kingdom.

Paul boasts in his weakness so that he can be truly strengthened in Christ (see 2 Cor. 12:9). In Jesus, the most powerful man who ever lived, we see gentleness, meekness, and vulnerability exercised in accordance with the three virtues of faith, hope, and love. Never once was he unmanly.

Billy Crystal's character Harry Burns is a stereotype: a man with a raging sex drive who stereotypes all women as objects of his desire. This is crass, and most readers will be offended by such a view. However, much Christian writing has reduced us in this same way, constantly depicting cross-sex interaction as a potential threat to sexual purity. Rather than upholding a call to healthy relationships between the sexes, we draw unreasonable lines, ostensibly to protect us, that uphold Harry Burns's reduction of men and women to their sexual potential.

We will get into the topics of purity and proper discernment in chapters 4 and 5, but for now let me say that imposing extrabiblical restrictions on all believers hinders spiritual growth and does not promote purity. Paul's words to the Colossians apply here.

> If you have died with Christ to the elementary principles of the world, why, as if you were living in the world, do you submit yourself to decrees, such as, "Do not handle, do not taste, do not touch!" (which all refer to things destined to perish with use)—in accordance with the commandments and teachings of men? These are matters which have, to be sure, the appearance of wisdom in self-made religion and self-abasement and severe treatment of the body, but are of no value against fleshly indulgence. (Col. 2:20–23)

We are to strive for real wisdom, not the appearance of wisdom. We are to live according to who we are. Real wisdom will discern that pharisaical hard and fast rules give only faux safety and faux friendship.

> When we impose cheap guilt-laden law on the body of Christ, even with the best of intentions, we end up enticing the forbidden. By telling adults that they can't interact, especially through text without a baby sitter, we turn every single encounter with one another into a brush with the forbidden. By our rules, we entice lust because we stop looking at one another as brothers and sisters in Christ who are image bearers, and instead unintentionally train ourselves to view one another as sex objects who can't possibly keep it in our pants long enough to have a God-honoring friendship.[20]

20. Sarah Taras and Jon Wymer, "Affairs Don't Start with Texts," *Just One Train Wreck after Another* (blog), March 20, 2017, https://timfall.wordpress.com/2017/03/20/affairs-dont-start-for-with-texts/.

Let's be careful not to make blanket judgments that cross-sex texting or emailing are signs that an affair is imminent. Reductive behaviors demean both men and women and inhibit our call to grow in Christ and love one another. I can't tell you how many times I have felt less like a human being, a sister in Christ, and more like a threat. This is humiliating and wrong.

Let's not reduce our brothers and sisters in Christ to stereotypes.

Holistic People, Holistic Church

Femininity benefits masculinity, and vice versa. When we view one another holistically, we reap the benefits of seeing people as Christ does, as well as growing through our interactions. Men learn a whole different aspect of brotherhood when they have sisters. Likewise, women cannot get a complete picture of what it means to be a sister without having brothers. Not only do we need to look at individuals holistically, considering all their faculties that make up the image of God, but we also need to look at the entire household of God holistically, considering how the minds, bodies, and souls of all his people hold fellowship in the framework of love and communion.

Discussion Questions

1. When we use "sanctified language" such as "unnecessary temptation," "protecting our purity," or "honoring our spouses" as an argument against friendship between the sexes, what are we really saying about (1) friendship and (2) the other sex? How is this language both manipulative and reductive?

2. As we consider a holistic answer to who we are and why that matters, how does our sexuality matter in all our relationships—not just our romantic ones?
3. What dysfunctional stereotypes of men and women might be affecting the way you relate to others? What would you change in your interactions and relationships if you viewed them more holistically? What can you do today to begin implementing this?

3

We Don't Know Our Mission

As we're seeing, our understanding of human identity—our anthropology—is a crucial factor in influencing how we will view the possibility of friendship between men and women. The sweeping proclamation that men and women cannot be friends because "the sex part always gets in the way" is a statement about our very selves. Billy Crystal's character has a valid point . . . if we adopt a worldly way of thinking about love and pleasure. But if we look at it from a theological perspective, we see that it not only reduces the sexes to their ability to provide sexual pleasure but also diminishes God's eternal purposes for men and women in our relationships both with him and with each other. We need to grasp that mission in order to pursue the communion that he has called us to, even while living under the struggles on our way there.

What is that mission? We are created for communion with the Triune God and with one another, as I noted at the end of chapter 1. Our sexuality is expressed in more places than the bedroom. In particular, Scripture shows that it is expressed as we live as brothers and sisters in relationship. We will get more into those details later on, but first we must explore this holy communion with the triune God, since all other loving communion flows from it. How does God initiate this holy communion with his people? And what is our role in it? Communion takes more than one person, so we need to evaluate our own participation.

As he lays the groundwork for his theological anthropology, Kelly Kapic writes that in revelation "we discover the Triune Creator, the human creature, and the particular call and response that hold together this Lord and his image bearers, by looking to the incarnate Christ."[1] What is this "call and response" between the creature and the Triune Creator? I propose that it is a liturgy that initiates our covenant communion.

Imagine if, as some people believe, we had a God who did not speak. If this were the case, we would never know the mission for which he has created us. The blessed truth is that God does communicate with his people, revealing who he is, who we are, and the terms and conditions of our relationship—our covenant. God has spoken! It's true, whether you believe it or not. But how does God speak to us? Should we be afraid? What should our response be?

How Does God Speak to Us?

The book of Hebrews starts with what I call the all-time best opening hook for a sermon ever:

Long ago, at many times and in many ways, God spoke to our fathers by the prophets, but in these last days he has spoken to us by his Son, whom he appointed the heir of

---

1. Kelly M. Kapic, "Anthropology," in *Christian Dogmatics: Reformed Theology for the Church Catholic*, ed. Michael Allen and Scott R. Swain (Grand Rapids: Baker Academic, 2016), 166.

all things, through whom also he created the world. He is the radiance of the glory of God and the exact imprint of his nature, and he upholds the universe by the word of his power. (Heb. 1:1–3 ESV)

This opening is full of contrasts, as Karen Jobes describes.

The contrast between the ages ("in the past" versus "these last days"), the audience ("our ancestors" versus "us"), and the mode of revelation ("prophets" versus "the Son") highlights the one concept that has remained the same through all time: *God has spoken to humankind.* The author of Hebrews opens his sermon with the bedrock of all biblical thought. *God has revealed himself to us.*[2]

If the holy, triune God has spoken to mankind, that changes everything. We must respond. But many people try to run away from this truth. Others try to soften and romanticize it, imagining that God speaks small messages to them every day—new revelations that are personally communicated. The first question recorded in Scripture challenges whether God has revealed himself truly at all: "Did God actually say . . . ?" (Gen. 3:1 ESV).

Throughout the book of Hebrews, the writer does something quite interesting—ascribing Old Testament quotations from Moses, David, Nathan, and Jeremiah to God the Father, Jesus Christ, and the Spirit. What does this kind of switcheroo of attribution tell us? It means that we too find God's Word to us in the Old Testament—just as much as we do in the New Testament.[3]

Since Hebrews starts by telling us that in "the last days" of

2. Karen H. Jobes, *Letters to the Church: A Survey of Hebrews and the General Epistles* (Grand Rapids: Zondervan, 2011), 63–64.

3. See Jobes, 71–72.

this age God has spoken "by the Son" (see Heb. 1:1), we would expect to see this thesis followed with a bunch of quotes from Jesus. But there are none! Jobes says that this is yet another purposeful, glaring contrast.

> Where the words of the prophets were the message from God in the past, the Son *himself* is God's final revelation. This is not to say that what Jesus said isn't important. It is to say that the *identity* of Jesus as the divine Son of God is what makes him the perfect and final revelation of God. . . . Jesus doesn't just speak God's words (that is what the prophets did), he *is* God's word.[4]

This is good news for us! God has revealed himself to us in Jesus Christ.

Jobes points out that, "because God's verbal revelation was at the heart of the fall, God's verbal revelation is also at the heart of redemption."[5] If God has spoken to us, then we must respond by obedience in faith. But what does that look like?

Call and Response

Have you ever had that dream that you went to school or to work, only to discover you were naked? Why do so many people have that dream? Dream analysts postulate that we are afraid of being exposed or that we feel accountable about something. This dream provokes panic and shame. Hopefully, we are good dream ninjas who can get out of the situation without being noticed. If someone called us out by name, that would be dreadful—even in a dream!

4. Jobes, 75–76.
5. Jobes, 65.

Well, Adam and Eve lived that dream. One minute they were naked and unashamed, living righteous lives in perfect communion with the holy God. Then Satan questioned God's words, and God's character behind them, and the woman delighted, desired, and took the forbidden fruit with her husband. "The eyes of both of them were opened, and they knew that they were naked; and they sewed fig leaves together and made themselves loin coverings" (Gen. 3:7). But the coverings were not enough. They were still exposed. Hoping to escape the Lord God, the man and his wife hid themselves.

"Then the LORD God called to the man, and said to him, 'Where are you?'" (Gen. 3:9).

Dale Carnegie, author of *How to Win Friends and Influence People*, popularized the notion that speaking someone's name is the sweetest sound they will hear. This is often true—unless it is the most terrifying sound they will hear. Have you ever been summoned when you've been busted? Or when you were hoping that the teacher wouldn't call on you? Being called out by name can be either wondrous or horrifying.

There is no hiding from the Lord God when he calls. When we read Genesis 3, we know that God knows where Adam and Eve are. He isn't asking them for their location but instead giving a divine call that initiates a response.

In this liturgy, what ought that response to be? The Hebrew question "Where are you?" ("*Ayyekkah?*") is to be answered, "Here I am!" ("*Hineni!*").[6] This reply is a yes to God, meaning "I am ready" or "at your service." It acknowledges that God is Creator and Lord and that the responder is his creature. It is a response of faith that becomes a continual liturgy throughout Scripture. God calls Abraham by name, and it

---

6. See Lawrence Troster, "Here I Am: Responding to the Call in Creation," Jewcology, November 20, 2011, http://jewcology.org/2011/11/here-i-am-responding -to-the-call-in-creation/.

was a sweet sound to his ears: "Here I am" (Gen. 22:1). When God tells Abraham to offer Isaac, his only son, as a burnt offering, Abraham proves that he meant his response, and by faith he brings Isaac all the way to the altar before he hears that sweet sound again. This time the angel of the Lord calls his name twice: "'Abraham, Abraham!' And he said, 'Here I am'" (Gen. 22:11). The Lord then provides a ram as the sacrifice in place of Isaac. Jacob responds to God's summons twice with "Here I am" (Gen. 31:11; 46:2). Moses, Samuel, and Isaiah also respond, "Here I am" to God (Ex. 3:4; 1 Sam. 3:1–10; Isa. 6:8). *Hineni. I'm at your service.*

But Adam and Eve do not answer in faith. Where are they? They are in sin. They are in unrighteousness. They are without a proper covering. The man turns on the women to blame her. Their communion with both God and each other is broken. Mission failed.

What is God's response to the first sin? In grace God calls out to Adam and Eve with the question *Where are you?*, pushing them to confess their sin. He shows them that their coverings are inadequate and that death is required to atone for sin. But God himself clothes them in animal skins. By providing clothing for Adam and Eve, he proclaims the *protoevangelium*— the first gospel (see Gen. 3:15). This is our first glimmer of the Christ who is to come, "the Son of the living God" (Matt. 16:16), "even He who comes into the world" (John 11:27).

Due to sin and the fall, we cannot come before the holy, good God clothed in our own righteousness. We are like Adam and Eve, hiding as God asks, "Where are you?" We are lost! We need another to answer that call for us, one who can stand before a holy God. Praise be to God that Jesus the Christ has answered, "Here am I, and the children God has given me" (Heb. 2:13 NIV). He has done what no man can do so that we too can answer the call.

Don't you hate when someone asks you, "Will you do me a favor?" There you are, trapped, put on the spot, as you don't know what that favor is or whether you are willing to do it. Sometimes we say, "Depends on what it is . . ." Sometimes we put our loyalty out there and just say, "Yes." Abraham, Jacob, Moses, Samuel, and Isaiah said yes to God's summons, and the following call on their lives was so difficult that they never could have come through on their own strength. We can't answer God's call appropriately without the gift of faith. God provides even the faith that we need, by his Spirit and in his Son, to respond.

Those who are not in Christ will also have to answer the call. But they will not be able to stand under the wrath of a holy God in their sin. He will respond with eternal judgment when that day comes.

The Ultimate Response That We Rest In

God calls us personally, by name, so *Here I am* is a personal response. But he does not call us alone, so *Here I am* is also a covenantal response. We are not autonomous beings—we were made for communion with God and others. We aren't just individual selves but "covenantal selves"[7] who are summoned by the great King. We can easily get caught up in our own stories, but God has cast us into his great drama.

This is the blessing that we didn't know we wanted: to have ears to hear the call and the faith to respond, "At your service!" This is our mission as human creatures. This is our "dignity and struggle, universality and particularity, relational and personal identity, all understood within the framework

---

7. See Michael Horton, *The Christian Faith: A Systematic Theology for Pilgrims on the Way* (Grand Rapids: Zondervan, 2011), 405.

of love and communion."[8] "To be human," Michael Horton writes, "is to be called by God to direct the whole creation to its appointed goal."[9]

What is the appointed goal for creation? It is to "[share] in God's Sabbath consummation."[10] We were made to rest in Christ, the Lord of the Sabbath (see Mark 2:27–28), the one in whom we find our ultimate satisfaction. We rest in Christ alone now for our salvation. But that is just the beginning. Our salvation has an appointed goal. We also rest in Christ for a fighting faith to persevere to the new heavens and the new earth of the resurrection when he returns. But what do we anticipate on that great Day of consummation, when we will finally rest for all our striving in faith to make it there? What will our heavenly repose be like? When our ultimate satisfaction is consummated, when the Groom returns for his bride, all God's people will bear his image perfectly, wor-shiping, serving, and living out vocations in perfect love and communion.

Do you hear God's call? *Where are you?* Are you hiding? Look to the incarnate Christ, who presents us before the Father holy and unblemished. Confess your sin and turn away from it as you turn to him and receive his righteousness. Join in the great response when you wake up, when you eat, work, and play, and when you lay your head down at night. *Here I am! Here we are!*

Amazingly, God also responds, "Here am I" when we call to him (see Isa. 52:6; 58:6–9; 65:1). How wondrous is it that our Lord serves us? This call doesn't leave us where we are, but creates new life, doing its work every day to transform us into the likeness of the Son.

---

8. Kapic, "Anthropology," 166.
9. Horton, *The Christian Faith*, 405.
10. Horton, 405.

The Weekly Call

We saw from Hebrews that God has spoken through the Old Testament prophets and now speaks through his Son in the Word, which is living and active (see Heb. 4:12). He has also established a liturgy—a corporate, weekly call—to lead us in a covenant renewal ceremony of worship. Each week he asks us where we are.

How do you respond to the weekly call? *Lord, I'm weary from trying to be a good person all week. My kids are needy. I'm behind with work. I have a deadline, you know. I would just like one day to sleep in and have some "me" time. Besides, if I go today, I know I'm going to run into (fill in the blank), and I just can't handle him at the moment. Even worse, I might get asked to do something, and Lord, I've got nothing left.* Go ahead and confess this if it is where you are. But remember *who* you are.

When we worship, we don't just walk into a building and go through some holy motions. We are summoned by our mighty God to receive Christ and all his blessings through the gifts of the ministry of Word and sacrament. This divine liturgy of call and response becomes very real to us, and we are able to glimpse something amazing. During Sunday worship, believers get a taste of the heavenly worship that is to come. There is a sense in which our future reality of the new creation is breaking into our current lives in the present during corporate worship.

Where have you been? You've been declared holy and righteous, but every day you struggle to live out that reality in a world subjected to the curse of sin. You've groaned with creation, *How long, O Lord, until you come to consummate this union in the new heavens and the new earth? How long will I have to continue to battle with sin?* And you are empowered by the Holy Spirit to do just that.

If we look within ourselves, we won't find the rest we so desperately need. The Spirit doesn't work apart from his Word. We need to hear God's Word spoken to us, and, when we do, it changes us. And so we respond, "Here I am." We come out from the world and our common vocations to a holy space filled with holy people, and there we receive Christ and all his blessings. We are weary of our own words, our family's words, and our neighbors' words. We need to hear the Word of God that gives us life. "Created by speech, upheld by speech, redeemed by speech, and one day glorified by speech, we are, like the rest of creation, summoned beings, not autonomous," Horton writes. "We exist because we have been spoken into existence, and we persist in time because the Spirit ensures that the Father's speaking, in the Son, will not return void."[11] That's what we need—the Father's speaking in the Son.

So we come. We are here. The preacher speaks for God and gives a call to worship. Look around! What do you see? Who joins with you in song, prayer, confession of sin, assurance of pardon, and responsive reading? An entire household of God—people of all ages, educational choices, job positions, political parties, sexes, ethnicities, levels of ability, and marital statuses . . . we are all God's people, called to communion with him and one another as sacred siblings.[12] We have all responded to the call. He has brought us together. What a peculiar bunch we are. But we have something unifying in common: we are all God's people, and we are on a mission.

---

11. Michael S. Horton, *People and Place: A Covenant Ecclesiology* (Louisville: Westminster John Knox Press, 2008), 61.

12. I first saw this term used in Sue Edwards, Kelley Mathews, and Henry J. Rogers, *Mixed Ministry: Working Together as Brothers and Sisters in an Oversexed Society* (Grand Rapids: Kregel, 2008).

"Agency and Purpose Matter"[13]

We were not designed to be isolated worshipers of God. We were designed "for communion with God, neighbor, and the earth."[14] This changes the way that we think about our whole beings. Reoriented, "we see [our bodies and their faculties] relationally rather than reductively."[15] We find our purpose in Scripture. The command "You shall love the LORD your God with all your heart and with all your soul and with all your might" (Deut. 6:5) encapsulates the heart of being human. It is the call for all mankind to order all our faculties toward the purpose for which we were created. Jesus confirms this.

> "You shall love the Lord your God with all your heart, and with all your soul, and with all your mind." This is the great and foremost commandment. The second is like it, "You shall love your neighbor as yourself." (Matt. 22:37–39)

"This call to 'love God' was a call to be truly and freely a human creature, created 'very good' so as to enjoy harmonious relations with the Creator and the rest of his creation."[16] We have been created for loving communion with the triune God and our neighbors, and we have been given agency to do that with our hearts, souls, and minds.

While the first Adam's sin affected the "entire world (Rom. 5:12–14), so Jesus's life-giving reality, which has overcome death itself, now promises to affect the entire cosmos (Rom. 5:15–21)."[17] Do we believe this or not? We were created for

13. Kapic, "Anthropology," 177.
14. Kapic, 177.
15. Kapic, 178.
16. Kapic, 178.
17. Kapic, 180.

communion with God and others; therefore we long for it. But do we think that, while Jesus' death secured our salvation and eternal life, our communion with him has no direct correlation to our communion with others and this world? If we believe the excuses for why Christian men and women can't be friends, we deny both our purpose (communion) and our agency to achieve it.

Do we have the faculties to enjoy relationships between the sexes in purity? How does our communion with God affect our communion with our neighbors? Does it cause us to exclude the other sex from our friendships? Do we express our love for one another by *not* being friends? Is *that* our agency and purpose while we wait around for the Lord's return? Is that how we promote one another's holiness? Or, leading to our next chapter, should we expect relational growth?

Along with our brothers and sisters, we are headed toward a communion with the triune God that we get only a taste of now. As Michael Horton says, we are summoned beings, and our aim is to direct all creation to its appointed end. When we know who we are and can answer that divine liturgical call, we know that our covenant identity puts us in a family with other blessed people.

We find meaning and identity not by looking within ourselves but by directing our gaze to our Creator and Lord—the "divine Other,"[18] whose image we bear. I'm just going to let Horton play us out of this chapter, because I continually return to his description of covenant identity as I long to be wise about living in light of who God is and who I am.

> It is only as we take our place in this theater of creation—
> the liturgy of God's speaking and creaturely response—that

18. Horton, *The Christian Faith*, 405.

we discover a selfhood and personhood that is neither autonomous nor illusory but doxological and real. Who am I? I am one who exists as a result of being spoken by God. Furthermore, I am one of God's covenant children whom he delivered out of Egypt, sin, and death. I am one who has heard his command but not fulfilled it, one in whom faith has been born by the Spirit through the proclamation of the gospel. Because human beings are by nature created in covenant with God, self-identity itself depends on one's relation to God. It is not because I think, feel, experience, express, observe, or will, but because in the totality of my existence I hear God's command and promise that I recognize that I am, with my fellow image-bearers, a real self who stands in relation to God and the rest of creation.

No one can escape the reality of God in his or her experience, because there is no human existence that is possible or actual apart from the ineradicable covenant identity that belongs to us all, whether we flee the summons or whether we reply, "Here I am."[19]

Discussion Questions

1. Have you ever thought about the significance of your humanness as one called by God to direct the whole creation to its appointed goal, which is nothing less than sharing in God's Sabbath consummation? What is your response to this call? Why is Sunday worship vital to this call? Why is friendship?

2. How does the command to love God and neighbor call us to true freedom? What would it look like if we

19. Horton, 405–6.

over-sexualized the intimacy of this command to love God and neighbor? What would it look like if we withheld appropriate intimacy?

3. Where are you? If your appointed goal is eternal communion with the triune God and other people, how does your life reflect that now (1) in your view of the church and corporate worship, (2) in your prayer life and time in the Word, and (3) in your relationships with both believers and nonbelievers?

4

We Misunderstand the
Nature of Purity

We all agree that Christians should care for purity. I whole-heartedly advocate sexual purity and would never want to influence anyone into promiscuity or sexual sin of any kind. But what should be a basic conviction of the Christian faith has become its own movement that focuses on our sexual desires as key to our identity. From adolescence, many Christians are encouraged to kiss dating goodbye[1] and sign pledges of purity, while participating in organizations such as True Love Waits and Silver Ring Thing.

Much of the language coming out of these movements and books sounds biblical and virtuous, and these organizations have admirable zeal for providing good models and teaching for teenagers. But a closer examination of the teaching coming out of the purity movement reveals that we need more

---

1. See Joshua Harris, *I Kissed Dating Goodbye: A New Attitude Toward Romance and Relationships* (Colorado Springs: Multnomah, 1997).

than good motives for promoting purity. If we merely react to culture without a proper theology of purity, we rip purity out of its context of Christian holiness and the local church's disciple-making commission and inadvertently market it as an ideological commodity couched in the psychological language of today's secular world.[2]

A major language shift has taken place, and our thinking is changing with it. Evangelicals in the purity culture have moved from discussing sexual behavior as a fruit and out-working of being made in the image of God and of Christian holiness, to focusing on sexual purity commitments as the core of our identity. Even dating has moved from being an activity to a status—one that "pure" people are encouraged to avoid.

Many of us have been shaped by the purity movement, directly or indirectly. We have a false notion of what purity is and how it functions. Otherwise sensible men and women are afraid of one another. Our "purity" is our orthodoxy.

Now the movement is old enough that we are beginning to hear from the adults who committed to it as teens and are paying the consequences.[3] Zealous to protect their purity, many have put such a weight on sexual temptation and have sexualized their peers to such a degree that, having never been on dates or developed cross-sex friendships, they haven't found the perfect spouse they were promised. Others have rushed into courtships that ended in divorce and are ashamed of their failure in this whole Christian purity venture. Some have left the church altogether because they entered Christianity

2. For a fascinating read on this subject, see Sara Moslener, *Virgin Nation: Sexual Purity and American Adolescence* (New York: Oxford University Press, 2015).
3. See Thomas Umstattd Jr., "Why Courtship is Fundamentally Flawed," *Thomas Umstattd* (blog), August 12, 2014, http://www.thomasumstattd.com/2014/08/courtship-fundamentally-flawed/.

through the purity movement and associate it with the faith. Singlehood seems like a cruel judgment on someone's inability to land a mate, rather than a dignified status for a chaste person who is wholeheartedly committed to God. Some people are so pure that they're painfully alone, cut off from even godly, meaningful cross-sex friendships and companionship.

Is "purity" a worthy accomplishment when it separates one from the joy of Christian fellowship?

"Relational Growth Matters"[4]

Hindsight reveals the damage that well-intentioned purity movements have done by not grasping the comprehensiveness of biblical purity. Purity is not a static state that holds something back and waits for a change in marital status, it's not a great exchange for marital bliss and the safety of our society, and it's not an individualistic expression or path to self-improvement. Purity is relational and giving, never stagnant and passive.

When God made man and woman in his image, he pronounced his creation "very good." What does this mean? What did God expect from this goodness? Did he create man and woman, declare them good, and then leave things alone, as if goodness is static and passive? Or does Adam and Eve's goodness also point to how they were equipped to actively cultivate and expand all that he had given them in their lives together? Kelly Kapic argues that God's declaration shows a "dynamic or relational view of the human person. . . . Just as God planted the garden to grow, so he planted Adam in the midst of that garden—*to grow*. . . . We were created good

4. Kelly M. Kapic, "Anthropology," from *Christian Dogmatics: Reformed Theology for the Church Catholic*, ed. Michael Allen and Scott R. Swain (Grand Rapids: Baker Academic, 2016), 181.

with the expectation of growing in that goodness."[5] This point is key.

God's declaration communicates that humanity was "rightly ordered and properly placed within the structure of God's overall creation. Such goodness consisted in their loving communion with the Creator, a relationship that would foster human flourishing and joy."[6] We looked at this in the last chapter. What a blessing to be created for a loving fellowship with God and one another! This is goodness! God has created us for this growth in knowledge of who he is, what he has done, and what he is doing for us. And God calls us to glorify him, to our own benefit. The more we learn of him, the more our joy increases and leads us to praise. When we love God, we love what he loves. This eradicates any racism, sexism, ageism, classism, or any other reductive behavior among us.

Relational growth not only matters but is also a great blessing. Fundamentally, relationships involve a forward direction of growth and discovery through communion. Relationships are not static. Since God is our divine Creator, our communion with him not only reveals more about who he is but also reveals more about who we are. We were made to enjoy his love, and we were made to share in that love. This intimacy distinguishes humanity from the rest of creation.[7]

What Purity Looks Like

Now, let's think about the implications of relational growth for purity and coed friendships. Christians often warn against friendships between men and women because—and I whisper—"the sex part always gets in the way." But the very

5. Kapic, 181.
6. Kapic, 182.
7. See Kapic, 182.

definition of a friendship is platonic: "intimate and affectionate, but not sexual."[8] How can we grow relationally if we separate ourselves from our brothers and sisters?

A commenter on Twitter asked me a question that basically put a Christian spin on the Billy Crystal teaching: when would it be beneficial to have a friend of the other sex? Really, she was asking whether coed friendship is even possible. What is our answer? Do we say before one another in God's household and the watching world, "No, on this side of the resurrection, friendship is not possible"? What does purity look like in coed friendships? Avoidance?

A flood of examples of beneficial coed friendship immediately comes to mind: work situations, neighborly situations, community outreach situations, and parenting situations. But, beyond that, shouldn't we already have a baseline level of friendship established? Paul calls Timothy to treat "the older women as mothers, and the younger women as sisters, in all purity" (1 Tim. 5:2). We know how to do this! We know how to promote holiness in brother-sister relationships.

I have a close relationship with my brother. When we married, things did change. Our spouses get the main focus of our attention and time, because our marriages are unique and exclusive unions that we uphold and promote for each other. My brother and I don't try to exclude our spouses when we spend time together. Our brother-sister relationship has matured and is not the same as it used to be, but it certainly wasn't stunted by our marriages. And when we do happen to be alone together, it's not a threat to our marriages. Our friendship benefits our marriages; it does not subvert them.

The church has fought to promote purity in a culture that

---

8. *Oxford English Living Dictionaries*, s.v. "platonic," accessed May 19, 2017, https://en.oxforddictionaries.com/definition/platonic.

is enraptured by the sexual revolution. So it seems strange that we have also overly sexualized the concept of purity. Much of what is taught about purity in contemporary Christian literature treats it as something that can be taken away, something that needs to be guarded until the proper time. Young men and women are taught that their purity is a gift to be given on their wedding day. Until then, they are to protect this purity. Christians are taught that if they can just maintain a pure (read "virgin") status in their singlehood, they will be rewarded greatly with a fulfilling marriage. It's a great exchange: your purity for blessed communion with your soul mate. Then all your longings will be satisfied. Then you will be complete.

But this is a cruel teaching. Singles are left feeling like they are not whole or able to be fulfilled in the Christian life—like they are stuck in relational stagnation. Not only that, their interactions with the other sex are suspect. Intense weight is laid on what should be considered casual activity. Something as basic as having coffee with someone carries the pressure of ascertaining whether they are marriage material—as if marriage is the only product of relational growth. A stimulating conversation with another person's spouse is deemed inappropriate. Many singles feel that they are without a place in the church. They want to be known, to have intimate interaction, and to belong somewhere. They want to know that they are protected and valued, that someone's got their back. Sometimes the church tries to accommodate them by providing a singles ministry. But they often function as a sanctified meat market—a place to shop for a husband or wife. All the while, the young women are encouraged to wear their purity rings—like a seal of quality for any consumers who want a guaranteed product.

Additionally, this mind-set promotes the false expectation that marriage will fulfill all your needs for companionship and growth—sexual, emotional, and intellectual. We know this isn't true, which is why we are so guarded in fostering friendship between the sexes. Yet we hold up the nuclear family as the ideal haven in which we find our rest. Many Christians discover that they can be just as lonely, if not more, in a marriage.

In his book *Strangers in a Strange Land*, Archbishop Charles Chaput uses similar language to Kapic when arguing that we must not be reductive when it comes to purity or preemptive against temptation to sin.

> Purity is about wholeness or integrity. It means that the body, mind, heart, and soul are rightly ordered toward God. Every element of who we are is doing its part to bring us to union with God, which is our ultimate happiness. Given the strength of the sexual desires we all feel, rightly acting on those desires is a key part of maintaining purity. For single people and celibates . . . it means offering those desires up to God and seeking to channel them in our love and service for others.[9]

Understanding purity is essential to relational growth. But much current teaching in the church actually prohibits relational growth. Purity isn't merely abstention. It isn't practiced by avoidance. Purity isn't just a physical status for a virgin, nor is it even the success of a faithful marriage. Purity is preeminently about our communion with God—a fountain that overflows into our other relationships.

This doesn't soften the warning against temptation but acknowledges and confesses it to God, so that we can see as he sees and love as he loves. Then our desires are rightly ordered. How beautiful is that? If purity is preeminently about

---

9. Charles J. Chaput, *Strangers in a Strange Land: Living the Catholic Faith in a Post-Christian World* (New York: Henry Holt, 2017), 180.

our communion with God, then we can pursue holiness in others and ourselves while abhorring sin.

Purifying Generosity

We rightly acknowledge that the flesh is still weak, even for brothers and sisters in Christ, and we need to address that. But the answer is not to remain weak. The Billy Crystal rule assumes that there's one category of so-called love and that it is always erotic, never platonic. The apostle John doesn't tell us to hold back our love, however, but to love our brothers and sisters with a *holy* love.

> Beloved, if God so loved us, we also ought to love one another. No one has seen God at any time; if we love one another, God abides in us, and His love is perfected in us. (1 John 4:11–12)

> There is no fear in love; but perfect love casts out fear, because fear involves punishment, and the one who fears is not perfected in love. We love, because He first loved us. (1 John 4:18–19)

> And we have this command from him: The one who loves God must also love his brother and sister. (1 John 4:21 csb)

We are to look to our ultimate hope, which is to be transformed into the likeness of Christ, even though we can't fully grasp what that will be. And this great hope is not merely wishful thinking; it is purifying.

> See how great a love the Father has bestowed on us, that we would be called children of God; and such we are. For

this reason the world does not know us, because it did not know Him. Beloved, now we are children of God, and it has not appeared as yet what we will be. We know that when He appears, we will be like Him, because we will see Him just as He is. And everyone who has this hope fixed on Him purifies himself, just as He is pure. (1 John 3:1–3)

Because we are adopted sons in the Son, and our hope lies in full glorification and Christlikeness, we are called to purify ourselves. What does that mean? We cannot do this without Christ, who is our purity. But what does *that* mean? It means that we don't purify ourselves through abstinence. We purify ourselves by fixing our hope on Jesus Christ, "for from Him and through Him and to Him are all things. To Him be the glory forever. Amen" (Rom. 11:36). Kapic builds off this verse in discussing the paradox of how Christians live under God's divine generosity as we belong to him.

> God's ownership is much more dynamic than we might expect. While we often associate the idea of "ownership" with locks and keys, safe deposit boxes, bank accounts, and home security systems, God's ownership is fundamentally different. Unlike us, God does not own by keeping, but by giving. . . .
>
> Since God did not create to satisfy any inadequacy or need of his own, but out of the fullness of his delight and love, this delight and love flow to the creatures as generosity and back to God as thanksgiving and praise. Creation reflects and therefore shares in—or "beholds"—God's great glory. Our good has by his hand become a means of God's ultimate glory, intrinsically connected (cf. Ezek. 36:22–27).
>
> The nature of this connection is a key to a healthy view of God and ourselves. As God's giving does not impoverish

but enriches him, so we, as we offer back to God the gifts he has given and sanctified in us, are enriched in his glory and are satisfied in and through him.[10]

The dynamic nature of God's generosity applies to our purity. Our purity is from God. Think of all that this purity entails. It involves our hearts and our thoughts, proper active love, integrity and holiness, and cleanliness, without being mixed with sin in body, mind, and soul. Can anyone uphold this in herself? Himself? No! But God graciously gave us his Son, imputing Jesus Christ's full righteousness to every believer. From him we are given everything that purity entails. Everything! And through him we remain pure.

Jesus didn't just pay for our impurity and give us his purity; he has given us the Holy Spirit! Paul makes this argument when discussing purity: "Do you not know that your body is a temple of the Holy Spirit who is in you, whom you have from God, and that you are not your own? For you have been bought with a price: therefore glorify God in your body" (1 Cor. 6:19–20). God has given the Holy Spirit to dwell within us—to tabernacle with us. Now that is holiness and purity! While affirming God's ownership of us, Paul tells us that God has given us himself. Talk about divine generosity! He then concludes that we are to glorify God in our bodies. Our purity is from God and through God, and we respond by offering it back to God. Purity isn't merely abstaining from sexual activity; it isn't even having sex within marriage. It is offering our whole selves back to the Giver.

All too often, Christ is viewed as a consolation prize when we are denied our desires. But we will not find our ultimate

10. Kelly M. Kapic, *God So Loved, He Gave: Entering the Moment of Divine Generosity* (Grand Rapids: Zondervan, 2010), 24–25.

satisfaction in sex, despite the lie that many believe when they entertain lustful thoughts, behave inappropriately, and participate in premarital or extramarital sex. Temptations to sexual sin must be confessed and offered to God. That too is an act of faith as we offer ourselves to the one who sustains us.

This is important for married people to understand. Often, as we've seen, abstinence teaching within the church focuses on man-centered gratification that has nothing to do with true purity. Purity is treated as a commodity for ultimate blessing: if you maintain your virginity until marriage, you will be blessed with wonderful sex and a happily-ever-after relationship. Don't be fooled—this is the prosperity gospel, in which God's holy standard exists only to reward you for your great victory. Many disillusioned Christians who tried to "do it the right way" have fallen hard when they didn't get the rapturous blessing they thought they had earned.

Our purity is from God, through God, and to God. We find our greatest satisfaction and joy in a positive response of gratitude and worship. The Lord has truly been victorious. He can sustain us in our weaknesses and give us his own power to love him and to hate sin. We can share in his love for his people with godly, appropriate affection, and all our affections will be returned to him in fullness of glory. He wants to give us the true pleasure that is to be found in blessed communion with the triune God and his people.

When we know and experience this, we do not put false expectations on others—even on our spouses. Instead we look at our brothers and sisters with the eyes of faith.

Purity Is Wise, Not Oppressive

Jesus Christ is our great treasure. We don't need a movement with pledge cards, customized Bibles, and silver rings.

We *do* need to live according to our eternal purpose, responding to God's call for us in our relationships. This brings up more practical questions about the common restrictions that men and women are encouraged to put in place as barriers to acts of friendship and as "protectors" of purity.

The twentieth-century Catholic philosopher Dietrich von Hildebrand refers to this kind of oppression as "the spell of a negative sexuality,"[11] because fleshly thinking and extra-biblical rules for sexual constraint totally miss the mark of apprehending purity. After all, one can avoid having an affair without truly embracing purity. While faithfulness in marriage is expected, it is not necessarily virtuous if it's due to perceived self-importance, an *un*sensuous temperament, or a lack of opportunity. As von Hildebrand teaches, purity is a virtue because it exists when one "freely cooperates in its production," and it "involves a habitual response to some value."[12] A virtue is a standard of goodness that compels us to act toward its attainment. Purity is a virtue because we are actively and freely responding to God's liturgical call for holy communion.

I am perplexed by some of the language people use in order to uphold strange guidelines for protecting purity in their marriages. A quadriplegic woman explained to me that several years ago some men had taken her to the hospital to visit her husband. She said she had experienced inappropriate feelings of attraction during this ride, and that this was a challenge to her purity. She concluded that she had done the wrong thing by accepting the ride.

But is this woman less pure because she felt attracted

11. Dietrich von Hildebrand, *In Defense of Purity* (Steubenville, OH: Hildebrand Press, 2017), 24. Originally published as *Reinheit und Jungfräulichkeit* (Köln: Oratoriums Verlag, 1927).
12. Hildebrand, 34.

to other men? It sounds to me like she acted rightly on her desires, maintaining her purity by offering them back to God through loving her husband well.

The woman also said that she feels loved and cherished because her husband will not offer a woman a ride or accept one himself. This comment is representative of how many other spouses think. But which person expresses more value for who we are in Christ and who our spouse is—someone who can't offer a service for a person in need because they can't deal with attraction, or someone who properly orients their affections in a godly way?

The real question to ask regarding purity is, *what do you most value?* Is it your career or ministry, and therefore you must guard against any appearance that may give people ammunition against your image? Do you value the perfect marriage, even at the expense of valuing others? (And what kind of marriage requires you to reduce all others of the other sex in order to value your spouse?) Or do you consider it most valuable to "[live], so to speak, in the sight . . . of God's purity, the fountainhead of all purity, and [to respond] to it with the permanent and habitual assent of his will"?[13] He is our treasure. Living a life in communion with God will help put all our other values in perspective. We will then have a clearer understanding of purity, marriage, sex, and appropriate relationships.

Von Hildebrand insists on purity as a positive virtue that "always lives in an attitude of reverence for God and His creation, and therefore reveres sex, its profundity, and its sublime and divinely ordained meaning."[14] The pure person embraces and treasures the sexual gift in marriage so as not to reduce it to

13. Hildebrand, 43.
14. Hildebrand, 40.

a base instinct. "The moment I treat physical sex as something complete in itself and take no account of its profoundest function, namely, in wedded love, I falsify its ultimate significance and become blind to the mystery it contains."[15] Reverence for God and a high view of sex also promote a corresponding response: we value others in their dignity as people made in the image of God.

The pure person does not behave prudishly, producing an "oppressive atmosphere" toward others, but "is distinguished by a limpid radiance of soul."[16] Those who oppress this beauty

> miss the peculiar freedom of the pure: the unconfined spirituality, the transparence, the radiance which is theirs alone. On the contrary, they are in bondage, their spirit is opaque and transmits no clear light, and they hang about every hole and corner in which sexuality lurks unbeknown. . . . Since they have never uprooted and overcome this attraction, nor even struggled against it in open combat, every other department of their life is infected and poisoned by this disposition.[17]

Those are strong words that we should let sink in for a minute.

While it may seem safe to impose rules that separate us from ordinary encounters with the other sex, this isn't the virtue of purity. It is overly sexualizing of others. Rejecting impurity or sexual transgression should never lead to rejecting the value of another person. The virtue of purity rightly orients sensuality before God and others. It perceives and responds to the holistic value in human beings.

15. Hildebrand, 7.
16. Hildebrand, 41.
17. Hildebrand, 24.

Our call to Christian love and fellowship as brothers and sisters doesn't call us to "the false modesty of the prude" but to a "humble sincerity."[18] Of course we promote one another's holiness, take sin seriously, and realize that we can easily fall into it. We don't think of a bunch of reasons to be alone with the other sex, we don't naively assume that everyone is safe, and we don't overestimate our own virtue. But, rather than creating extrabiblical rules, we are to do the hard work of rightly orienting our affections and exercising wisdom and discernment with others. We live before God in every situation. And in this manner, we will be able to perform ordinary acts of kindness and business without scandal.

One definition of pickpocketing points out that this method of larceny "may involve considerable dexterity and a knack for misdirection."[19] I see these unbiblical rules imposed on men and women as pickpocketing purity, stealing unearned virtue at the expense of another's dignity. Though I think that those who uphold the rules are the misdirected ones, wanting to exercise a virtue without noticing the positive work that they need to put in.

Discussion Questions

1. Have you absorbed any false notions of what purity is through evangelical movements or books? If so, how has that disoriented your identity?
2. What's the difference between negative sexuality and apprehending purity? Which approach helps us to grow relationally in goodness? Which approach is considered virtuous, and why?

18. Hildebrand, 42.
19. Wikipedia, s.v. "pickpocketing," last modified March 23, 2018, 23:37, https://en.wikipedia.org/wiki/Pickpocketing.

3. How has this chapter affected your views about purity? What positive effort can you put in to pursue purity in your relationships? What does sincere humility look like in relationships between the sexes, and how would that be distinguished from the false modesty of the prude?

5

We're Immature and Fearful

When I began cohosting a podcast with a seminary professor and a pastor, I was pleased that a woman had been invited to the table to talk about theology—and not just the pink passages—with the men. It was the first time I'd seen anything done like that in my circles, and so it was discouraging that some people were concerned that my presence would lead to impropriety. Someone said it would be different if I weighed three hundred pounds and had a mustache. (I guess it's okay to be superficial about attractive qualities when it comes to whom you will engage with in theological conversation?) This initial fearful response to my presence on the podcast reveals the immature thinking of many Christians when it comes to friendship between the sexes.

It's true that friendship, while innocent, should not be naive. In the very beginning, Adam and Eve show us the cost of entertaining bad company. Paul wrote, "Do not be deceived: 'Bad company corrupts good morals'" (1 Cor. 15:33). Christians who caution against friendship between the sexes warn against something very real: sin. But they let the fear of sinning reduce the virtue of friendship. Friendship isn't sin. But sin in friendship is devastating.

We've seen that we are called to communion: vertical communion with our creator God and horizontal communion with our brothers and sisters. Personal holiness is imperative for the first and foundational to the second. If we take sin lightly, we can't expect to have holy relationships, so any case for brother-sister relationships must include a call to spiritual maturity. A man and a woman can't be friends if one or both of them are deadlocked in immaturity and fear. Without spiritual maturity, we are back to catering to immature notions of sexuality.

"Sin Matters"[1]

Sin moved humanity from joyful communion with God to exile from God and subjection to his righteous condemnation. We must not downplay sin. Jeremiah Burroughs said, "It is a very evil choice for any soul under heaven to choose the least sin rather than the greatest affliction," and added, "There is more evil in sin . . . than in outward trouble in the world; more evil in sin than in all the miseries and torments of hell itself."[2]

When the first Adam—our federal representative—sinned, he plunged creation under the curse of God. Sin affected our bodies, minds, and souls so that they are not rightly ordered toward righteousness, love, and glory to God. Without Christ, we are unable to know Good and therefore unable to do good.

Sin's corruption is so saturating that it was necessary for Jesus to take on full and complete humanity in every part,

1. Kelly M. Kapic, "Anthropology," from *Christian Dogmatics: Reformed Theology for the Church Catholic*, ed. Michael Allen and Scott R. Swain (Grand Rapids: Baker Academic, 2016), 184.
2. Jeremiah Burroughs, *The Evil of Evils* (London, 1654; repr., Morgan, PA: Soli Deo Gloria reprint, 1992), 2–3.

only without sin. Christ's work was necessary for our salvation, and so is the Holy Spirit's work for our sanctification in body, mind, and soul.[3] God's people, by the powerful work of his Spirit, are called to a life of faith and obedience, so we are to always examine and test all things, holding fast to good while turning from evil (see 1 Thess. 5:21–22).[4]

It's important to realize that "sanctification does not come because we have hedged ourselves about with extra rules. Sanctification is the work of the Spirit in the heart which comes through the gospel, not the law."[5] The more familiar we are with God's Word, the more we will understand the principles behind his precepts. The law points us to Christ, and those who are in Christ will see his character in the law. The law teaches us holy living, but it does not give us the power or desire to obey. Christ does this through his Spirit working in us. Then we love his law and hate what works against it.

The law was never meant to save us. Many of the hard-and-fast rules that we add to protect ourselves work *against* Christ's sanctifying work, because they point to ourselves rather than to dependence on him. Wisdom and maturity know the difference.

A Desire for Holiness That Is Greater Than Our Fears

The idea that men and women can't be friends because the "sex part always gets in the way" has become so accepted that

3. Kapic, "Anthropology," 187.
4. For an exegesis of this Scripture arguing against those who use the KJV translation "abstain from all appearance of evil" as a way to support hard and fast rules, see Sam Powell, "Every Appearance of Evil, and the Billy Graham Rule," *My Only Comfort* (blog), April 14, 2017, https://myonlycomfort.com/2017/04/14/every-appearance-of-evil-and-the-billy-graham-rule/.
5. Sam Powell, "Billy Graham Rule Follow-up," *My Only Comfort* (blog), April

we think Billy Crystal was describing something normal—that normal friendship involves constant sexual desire. But, while we are susceptible to sin in this age, Christians know that sin will never be normal. It is an evil that works against our image bearing, and we are called and equipped to fight it. So, when Christians decide to avoid friendships with the other sex, they often do so with the good intention of avoiding sin.

Popular evangelist Billy Graham brought many men and women to the faith and tirelessly served God in spreading the gospel. There is so much we can commend about his legacy. But, with all the best intentions for upholding his holiness and faithfulness in his marriage, even Billy Graham bought into the notion behind the Billy Crystal rule. As public Christian figures, Graham and three other male leaders got together to make a list of resolutions that would help them to "avoid any situation that would have even the appearance of compromise or suspicion."[6] Other itinerant ministers who had fallen into sexual sin while away from their families deeply troubled these men and led them to this response. To flee from youthful lusts (2 Tim. 2:22), Graham strictly adhered to his new rules, saying that from that time on he would not "travel, meet, or eat alone with a woman other than [his] wife."[7] Over time, this personal rule that Graham made was embraced by many others as some kind of precedent to emulate.

It is honorable of leaders to carefully consider their influence on others and the effects of their actions on their ministry. But it's interesting to note that it's not *their* ministry—it's Christ's ministry. And Jesus did not use this guideline. His friendships

---

26, 2017, https://myonlycomfort.com/2017/04/26/billy-graham-rule-followup/.

6. Billy Graham, *Just As I Am* (New York: HarperOne, 1997), 128.

7. Graham, 128. However, he later admits to bending the rules a time or two, notably once when Hillary Clinton persuaded him that it would be okay for them to have lunch alone together in a public place "and still have a private conversation" (see p. 651).

with women were downright scandalous during his ministry on earth. At that time, women were not considered capable of the intimate communion of friendship. They were valuable to men for reproduction and sexual fulfillment only. A woman's sexual behavior determined her social status, and a woman's chastity was monitored with "suspicious observation."[8] Yet in Scripture we see Jesus accept invitations into women's homes, talk with women unaccompanied by a chaperone, travel with women, let a woman show affection for him, ask a woman for a drink and engage with her in theological discussion in the middle of the day where everyone could see, and trust women to be the first heralds of the gospel in an age when a woman's testimony was discounted. People whispered. They questioned his credibility because of his interactions with these women.

This same Jesus said that looking at a woman with lust is adulterous. This same Jesus preached about plucking out your eye if you keep using it to lust. He is serious about sin. Yet he doesn't pander to any of the superficial gender tropes or situational sociability structures imposed by the culture. So what was more important to Jesus: appearances or reality?

Additionally, even when emphasizing the evil of lust, Jesus doesn't say to pluck out the woman; he says to pluck out your eye. We are to use every part of our body to practice chastity instead of sin, and we pray for God to rightly order our desires. Christian leaders should certainly model chastity to us. But I would love to see chastity modeled with mature spirituality and godly friendship, not with suspicion and fear.

Our relationships tend to reveal the selfishness, jealousy, pride, complacency, and, yes, wrongly ordered affections and

---

8. See Kyle Harper, *From Shame to Sin: The Christian Transformation of Sexual Morality in Late Antiquity* (Cambridge, MA: Harvard University Press, 2016), 39–41.

lust that lurk in our hearts. Our relationships also confront us with the sins of those who we care about. It would be easier to isolate ourselves. But brothers and sisters in God's household are not called to immaturity and fear but called to promote one another's holiness (see Heb. 12:15–16).

What Distinguishes God's People?

What sets the church apart from the rest of the world? What does the world see when they look at us? We're a peculiar bunch, aren't we? But we have one thing in common: we are God's people. God's love should overflow from us toward one another. Peter pleads with Christians, on the grounds of their new life in Christ, "Since you have in obedience to the truth purified your souls for a sincere love of the brethren, fervently love one another from the heart" (1 Peter 1:22).

Our relationships are different from the world's. We have the eternal Word, and therefore we have an eternal, loving fellowship in it. "Earnest love within the Christian community [is] the hallmark of having been converted."[9] If you are born into a family full of siblings, you can't pretend you're an only child. It just doesn't work that way.

How does this jive with the Billy Crystal rule? It doesn't! We who have "tasted the kindness of the Lord" (1 Peter 2:3) are to "crave the Lord by adopting attitudes and behaviors that will sustain the new life [we] have begun by faith in Christ."[10] That includes "putting aside all malice and all deceit and hypocrisy and envy and all slander" (1 Peter 2:1). We aren't to present ourselves as Christians and not care about purity and holiness in our relationships. We aren't to be secret sinners.

And we should never tear one another down. "Righteous behavior toward one another defines love."[11]

Peter gives us the following exhortation:

> Beloved, I urge you as aliens and strangers to abstain from fleshly lusts which wage war against the soul. Keep your behavior excellent among the Gentiles, so that in the thing in which they slander you as evildoers, they may because of your good deeds, as they observe them, glorify God in the day of visitation. (1 Peter 2:11–12)

As a consequence of our exulted status as a "chosen race, a royal priesthood, a holy nation" (1 Peter 2:9), we are also aliens and strangers in these last days. We're peculiar to the world. Since we are set apart, others notice. We're not like them. We have a different allegiance, a different agency and purpose, and a different love. Because of this, we are called to suffering. Peter wrote to persecuted Christians who were dispersed throughout Rome. Like the nation of Israel, who also lived as aliens and foreigners, they were being watched. How they lived was a witness to who they were. But they had each other, and they were called to value this spiritual household.

We can't help but think of the metaphor that this language presents for Christians now. Wherever we are, this is not our final destination. We are headed for a new heavens and a new earth. We are called to live out who we are with integrity as we wait for the age that is to come. We are called to Christian maturity in relationships, even now, and this is also a witness to our neighbors. Will they see growth in the quality of our relationships? Will they see a sincere love for our Christian brothers and sisters? Will they notice that we are predictably

11. Jobes, 124.

absent from the activities of the common world on Sunday morning because we have answered the call to worship in our spiritual household? Will they see that, although we are like aliens in one sense, we stick together as a people?

Where Are Our Affections?

When Peter tells us to abstain from "fleshly lusts," he expects us to exercise the spiritual fruit of self-control in our relationships. He's not saying, "I know you can't help it. You're never going to get better, so please, just smile, give a polite greeting, and keep your distance. That way you can remain pure." No, he expects the sanctifying work of the Holy Spirit to affect how we behave and relate. He expects love! He expects us to look at one another and treat one another for who we are—"God's own possession" (1 Peter 2:9).

Where do you find yourself now? How are you responding to God's call on your life? We can't have mature friendships if we lack self-knowledge, purpose, and growth. As Christians, we have access to the true source of love as well as the direction of our own love. Remember, God calls every part of us—body, mind, and soul—to be properly ordered toward him. He wants to love us holistically, unlike Harry Burns, who doesn't want friendship with a woman except as a means to her body.

Identify Your Blind Spots

There are some practical self-evaluation questions we can ask ourselves to pinpoint exactly where are affections are oriented and to see whether we have any blind spots. These are important questions that help us to cultivate proper, holy affection. Avoidance is not purity. We are not being holy by avoiding any affection for the other sex. We need to deal with our affections in a mature, godly manner as we are called to love one another. Here are a few general pitfalls that keep us from the holy affection to which we are called.

Do you confuse attraction with temptation?

It's vital for us to be able to identify and orient our affections and our need for communion and friendship. When we long to be wanted and to have fellowship with someone who really knows us, we ought to look first to God. If we have a strong grasp of what it means to be human creatures, bearers of God's image for his glory and our good, and if we learn how to rightly orient ourselves in mature friendships, maybe we could prevent the marital affairs and scandals that happen even in the church.

When immature people have feelings for someone, they interpret them as sexual and romantic. But that is a reductive way to handle affection. Take the example of the quadriplegic woman in the last chapter. What if the feelings of attraction she experienced toward the men who had offered her a ride were the result of being appropriately cared for, leading her to feel something legitimate in response? This is a woman who is dependent on the care of a man—her husband. When, in his sudden absence, she is shown sincere kindness by other men, wouldn't she be *expected* to feel an emotional response to their help? Is it possible that we misread appropriate feelings due to the overly sexualized messages we hear, don't know how to recognize or maturely handle them, and resist the intimacy that we could experience as brothers and sisters?[12]

The truth is that we are attracted to more people than our spouses. Attraction is not impurity. Many things make a person attractive besides mere physical appearance. We should be attracted to godliness in a godly way. We can delight that

12. Thanks to my elder, Dave Myers, for this pertinent observation.

someone is attractive without impure thoughts figuring in. Finding someone attractive doesn't mean that we should pursue them romantically, however, or allow our thoughts to wander into sexual fantasy. That is self-absorption, not love. Love is so much more than romantic passion.

If we are weak in this area, or with a particular person, we should certainly not put ourselves in situations where we know we will stumble or cause a brother or sister to stumble. We should never feed temptation to sin. Doing so is a red flag that you are not genuine in godly fellowship.

Do you assume that you won't be tempted?

This is another sign of immaturity. Scripture tells us to expect temptation:

> Let him who thinks he stands take heed that he does not fall. No temptation has overtaken you but such as is common to man; and God is faithful, who will not allow you to be tempted beyond what you are able, but with the temptation will provide the way of escape also, so that you will be able to endure it. (1 Cor. 10:12–13)

We are tempted because of the sin in our own hearts. We need to offer it to the Lord as a sacrifice and properly orient our affections. We need to rehearse the truths of who we are and where we are, so that we can be obedient to that truth and purify our souls.

Do you expect marriage to fulfill all your relational needs?

Even those of us who are married should not orient all our affections toward our spouses. If we do this, we set ourselves up for failure by placing demands and expectations on our spouses that they cannot possibly fulfill.

It's also a bad idea for married people to compare their spouses to someone else, wishing that they had some of their qualities. We married the person who we married. Every marriage has ups and downs—and even moments when we think we'd be better off alone or with someone else. Most of the time,[13] this is where the rubber of faith needs to meet the road of obedience. We have the opportunity to grow closer to Christ as we grow in our love for and commitment to our spouses through tough times.

If our affections are properly oriented, the first place they will seek fulfillment is in answering our call to fellowship with the triune God. It is there that we will find satisfaction, because God is the fountain of love and he gives us his love as a fruit of the Spirit (Gal. 5:22). From that fountain, our affections will overflow to others with pure love.

A Call to Discernment and Wisdom

As we've seen, Scripture doesn't build fences between the sexes; it calls us to godly relationships. However, I am not dismissing real challenges between the sexes. Not all people are safe, so Scripture calls us to discernment and wisdom. When we discern, we separate truth from lies and error. We judge whether a person's actions are in harmony with who he or she claims to be. Discernment helps us to grow in Christlikeness.

> This I pray, that your love may abound still more and more in real knowledge and all discernment, so that you may approve the things that are excellent, in order to be sincere

13. Sadly, in some cases a spouse is abusive. If you are married to an abusive spouse or a spouse who struggles with addiction, you need to seek wise and mature brothers and sisters for help. If you are experiencing physical or sexual abuse, the police should be involved—but emotional and spiritual abuse can be just as damaging.

and blameless until the day of Christ; having been filled
with the fruit of righteousness which comes through Jesus
Christ, to the glory and praise of God. (Phil. 1:9–11)

Notice the "from him, through him, to him" language
here. Discernment is vital in all our relationships. Through
discernment, we recognize excellence, which is *from* Christ;
our righteousness is *through* him; and we offer the fruit of our
discernment back *to* him in praise and service. Through this,
we also reap the fruit of abounding love. Our relationships
are a gift from God, lived out before God and offered to God.
Therefore, we should never entertain inappropriate thoughts
or behaviors in any relationship. Our actions overflow from
our hearts. If we look to Christ and mature in his Word, we
will pursue Christlike relationships.

So we see that Scripture guides us to treat one another as
brothers and sisters in Christ, and it also warns us about false
and backslidden siblings. We need to know the difference, and
sometimes we do need to implement boundaries. For example,
we are wise to put boundaries on our interactions with a person like Harry Burns. Burns is a predator; he can't be a friend.

Harry Burns states his mission up front. Unfortunately,
some predators disguise themselves as spiritual leaders, thereby
gaining unchecked authority and trust. Some pastors abuse
their position to manipulate women who seek their counsel.
Because of this, many wise church leaders keep an open door
(or have a windowed door) when alone with a woman. They
do this not because women are a threat to their sexual purity
but because they want to assure those who trust them that
they are safe.[14] This is a kind gesture of leadership.

14. For a wise balance on situations such as this see Powell, "Billy Graham Rule
Follow-up." Of course, this doesn't mean that a closed door indicates that the pastor
is a predator or that the woman is trying to tempt him.

Not all Christians are mature, and none of us is fully matured. Often younger men and women, and especially teenagers, are not as mature with handling platonic relationships between the sexes as older Christians are. This does not mean that we should perpetually separate them from one another. But they do need guidance and modeling from their older brothers and sisters. Likewise, some adults are not in a good place to interact well within friendships. They may have sinful patterns, such as pornography addictions, that profoundly affect how they view men and women. Even people in your church may have become so caught up in sin and lust that they need extra pastoral care and accountability in their lives— maybe for a long period of time.

As we encourage godly relationships, we warn against sin. Our best guidance is the truth. Teenagers experience hormonal changes. Are we teaching them about purity, or merely how to avoid premarital sex? We may inadvertently provoke lust in them by focusing on and reducing them to their sexual urges. The secular world is already overly sexualizing our young men and women. We must come alongside our teens and young adults with biblical wisdom. Our goal isn't for them to merely avoid sin but for them to pursue holiness. Our goal is to teach them who they are and where they are, which profoundly shapes the way that they relate with others.

To show wisdom in relationships, we must also examine our own maturity and emotions. If you are married and find yourself romantically attracted to someone other than your spouse, or if you are single and find yourself romantically attracted to someone who is off limits for any reason, then you need to confess this to the Lord in prayer and not put yourself in situations that fuel romantic feelings. You may need to avoid car rides or eating together with this specific person. The same applies if you discern that others have inappropriate romantic feelings toward you. However, this doesn't mean that you need to apply a blanket rule against accepting rides from all friends.

Growth necessitates critical thinking and discernment. As you navigate your relationships, keep asking yourself, "Who am I? What is my purpose here?" If you find yourself struggling with an unhealthy attraction toward someone, this is a good time for self-evaluation. Why are you more vulnerable at this time? Are you currently experiencing some kind of emotional disappointment from someone else? Are you going through a lonely season? Is the sexual attraction an easy detour from God's call for you to give of yourself and pour yourself out on another's behalf?[15] The goal isn't *only* to avoid sin, but to refresh or nurture your position in Christ.[16]

If you are married and your spouse is uncomfortable with your friendship with someone, whether it's a man or a woman, listen to their reasons. Loving spouses are good at identifying unhealthy friendships. In my own marriage, I have noticed women whose intentions for my husband went beyond friendship. My husband heeded my discernment. Other times, my husband warned me about a girlfriend or two who showed manipulation and ungodly competitiveness in their friendships with me. He turned out to be right. Many areas in a friendship need discernment, and we can be blinkered by our own good intentions. If our spouses pick up on something that's off, we should listen to and honor them. Often they are right—and we don't ever want to make our spouses uncomfortable anyway.

Ultimately, much of our interaction with the other sex calls for some sanctified common sense. Sarah Taras and Jon Wymer's advice regarding our interactions calls for basic

---

15. Again, thanks to Dave Myers for some of these insights.
16. Thanks to Dave Myers for this line.

integrity: "Don't do in private what you wouldn't do in public."[17] For example, even though texting is a private activity, I am perfectly comfortable for my husband to read my texts, whether I'm writing to a man or a woman. There's nothing to hide when you treat people with common decency and respect.

Even sharing a meal in public with someone can increase intimacy. If we treat the intimacy appropriately as brother-sister intimacy, then everything stays properly platonic and our affections are rightly ordered. Most of us are able to do this. But if you are not, or if you find yourself in a vulnerable time or with someone who is not good company, make your decisions accordingly.

Temptation is real, and sin is evil. It may sound wise to avoid friendship between the sexes so that we can avoid sin. Yet we end up fearing disobedience more than having a zeal for *obedience*.[18] Growth matters. If we go out of our way to avoid meaningful relationships with the other sex, there is no growth. Completely avoiding any real engagement fools us into thinking that we're maturing when our relationships are actually becoming less mature.

When we avoid relationships with others, we are not dealing with the sin in our own hearts, confessing temptations, offering them to God, and choosing obedience and holy, purifying love. Doing these things is much more difficult than avoiding people.

Challenges should not be ignored. But they don't mean that we aren't called to intimate sibling communion with one another. They just mean that we need to grow. Plenty of naive

17. Sarah Taras and Jon Wymer, "Affairs Don't Start with Texts," *Just One Train Wreck after Another* (blog), March 20, 2017, https://timfall.wordpress.com /2017/03/20/affairs-dont-start-for-with-texts/.
18. See Paul M. Conner, *Celibate Love* (Huntington, IN: Our Sunday Visitor, 1979), 90.

Christians have committed sexual sin because they didn't give proper thought to the implications of who and where they were in their relationships. But cutting ourselves off from community doesn't prepare us for our eschatological hope. Let's do the work and experience the joy we are called to in maturity.

Discussion Questions

1. How is a love of God's law and a desire to obey him foundational to friendship? How can piling hard-and-fast rules on top of God's law work against Christ's sanctifying work for his people?
2. In what sense does the Billy Graham Rule intersect with the #MeToo movement? Consider what they are reacting against, the blanket messages they can send about men and women, the fear they provoke, and how they influence others.
3. Which best describes your own struggles with friendship between the sexes?
   a. You confuse attraction with temptation
   b. You assume that you won't be tempted
   c. You expect marriage to fulfill all your needs
   How can you work to become more mature, wise, and discerning in this area?

6

We've Forgotten What Friendship Really Is

What does *friendship* mean to you? Is erotic love in marriage the only real, valuable outlet for our affection? Does all affection lead to erotic love? While this whole book is working out a theology of friendship, we need to pinpoint more aspects of this elusive term.

The Netflix show *Stranger Things* takes us back to friendship in the '80s. Ah, the glorious '80s. Friendship is a major theme and is shown through a fraternal bond between twelve-year-old boys. They have a friendship code (they vow not to lie) and a definition of what a friend is (a friend never breaks a promise). Yet even these best of friends end up lying some as they risk their own lives for one another. Friendship can be tricky. But the show is so appealing because of the sacrifices these friends make for one another and the way they grow as a result.

Sadly, the adolescent boys of *Stranger Things* have a more noble view of friendship than many adults do today. Friendship has become both marketable and disposable. To increase sales, businesses target not only each of us ourselves but also the "friends" in our social media networks. And just look at how many we have! We've built empires of friends, which are all subject to our own customizing. I can accept you, mute you, block you, and retweet you. I can stalk you, favorite you, and hashtag you. I may never actually meet you, friend. And, of course, I can *un*friend you with one click. Social media presents a platform for networking and being friendly, but it is so disembodied that it easily feeds our propensity to isolate ourselves. I don't need to make sacrifices to be your so-called friend; I can just like your posts and comment at my convenience.

Can men and women be friends? At least when Harry Burns said they could not, it was because he knew that friendship had certain expectations he knew he would not be able to meet with a woman. He used friendship with a woman in order to seduce her, and he knew that wasn't right. But we are inconsistent about friendship. On the one hand, we have trivialized friendship through technology; on the other, we warn against *real* friendship between the sexes. On the one hand, any stranger can be our friend; on the other, we are suspicious and protective of those who *could* actually be close to us. Maybe we can take our cue from the *Stranger Things* boys, who said a couple of things about friendship and then spent the rest of the series showing what they meant. Here I will introduce what a friend is supposed to do. Part 2 of this book will describe the actual practices of friendship.

Friendship Is the School of Virtue in a Shared Pursuit

What is friendship? It isn't just some poetic ideology. Friendship is something that we do. To be a friend, we need to exercise virtue. Friendship requires moral excellence because it is not primarily for our own benefit but is formed through our sacrifices for another. Others-centered virtue creates a friendship that enhances the souls of all participants.

Friendship is not merely companionship. It is not merely recognizing affection for another person. "To the Ancients, Friendship seemed the happiest and most fully human of all loves; the crown of life and the school of virtue."[1] Friendship changes us.

Aelred of Rievaulx, an English Cistercian monk from the twelfth century, wrote of three different kinds of friendship: carnal, worldly, and spiritual. "The carnal is created by a conspiracy in vice, the worldly is enkindled by hope of gain, and the spiritual is cemented among the righteous by a likeness of lifestyles and interests."[2] Spiritual friendship[3] is the highest form of friendship because it is rooted in union with Christ and therefore has eternal value.[4] This spiritual friendship is a proper longing in our hearts that so often eludes us.

> Friendship is that virtue, therefore, through which by a covenant of sweetest love our very spirits are united, and *from many are made one.* Hence even the philosophers of this world placed friendship not among the accidents of mortal life but among the virtues that are eternal. Solomon seems to agree with them in this verse from Proverbs: *"a friend loves always."* So he obviously declares that friendship is

1. C. S. Lewis, *The Four Loves* (1960; repr., New York: Harcourt Brace, 1991), 57.

2. Aelred of Rievaulx, *Spiritual Friendship*, trans. Lawrence C. Braceland, ed. Marsha L. Dutton (Trappist, KY: Cistercian Publications, 2010), 62.

3. Some associate Aelred of Rievaulx with the contemporary Spiritual Friendship movement that has been popularized by Wesley Hill, a self-identifying gay celibate Christian. While I share Hill's enthusiasm for Aelred's work, I am interacting with Aelred outside the influence of that movement.

4. See Aelred, 41.

eternal if it is true, but if it ceases to exist, then although it seemed to exist, it was not true friendship.[5]

True friendship, or spiritual friendship, is not disposable. It is not friendship for friendship's sake. It is not self-seeking for advancement; it involves collaboration for something outside us. We find true friends by being virtuous people who live for truth in community. "Friendship must be about something. . . . Those who have nothing can share nothing; those who are going nowhere can have no fellow-travellers."[6] For this reason, spiritual friendship among those of us who are united in Christ is eternal and is the highest form of friendship. After all, we are fellow travelers to a new heavens and a new earth.

Because of God's common grace to all, we can share our pursuit and love of particular truths, giftings, and blessings with unbelievers in friendship as well. Whether we have a love of culinary arts, bird-watching, or fly-fishing, it is a delight to discover others who also care about our particular pursuits. Lewis describes the common beginning of a friendship in the expression "What? You too? I thought I was the only one."[7]

We don't necessarily hunt for friends; we discover them. Our common responsibilities, such as parenting and vocations, lead us to look for others who have an interest in the same truths that we do. As we pursue these interests, believers will promote virtue in every friendship, not only our Christian ones. And "mixed" friendships will challenge and sharpen us in our sanctification, even as we aim for the good of our unbelieving friends. If these friends never come to know the Lord, our friendship will not carry over to eternity, but the fruit of its training in virtue will.

5. Aelred, 59.
6. Lewis, *The Four Loves*, 66–67.
7. Lewis, 65.

In our common pursuits and joys, we learn more about people and develop an added bond of friendship and appreciation for them in a way that we never could by simply interviewing them to see how compatible we are with them.[8] The focus isn't on our friendship but on our interests. This is also what distinguishes friendship love from erotic love. "In some ways nothing is less like a Friendship than a love-affair. Lovers are always talking to one another about their love; Friends hardly ever about their Friendship."[9]

This is also why cross-gender friendships are more likely in some situations than in others.[10] Since my husband works in education and I work as a writer and speaker regarding theological issues, each of us is exposed to people of both sexes who share our interests. We don't seek friendship with the other sex just for the sake of it. And there are plenty of times when Matt needs time with the guys and I just want a night with the girls. But my friendships would be impoverished if I had only a sisterhood.

With some friendships we must be more guarded, as we evaluate people's maturity levels and where they are spiritually. But in the school of virtue that pursues truth, "the more righteous, chaste, and open it is, the more it is carefree, enjoyable, and happy. . . . Of course prudence guides, justice rules, strength protects, and temperance moderates this friendship."[11]

Aelred points to creation in order to teach us about the higher blessing of friendship. He doesn't see Eve's role as Adam's helper, or ally, exclusively as a teaching about marriage roles.

8. See Lewis, 71.
9. Lewis, 61.
10. See Lewis, 72–73.
11. Aelred, *Spiritual Friendship*, 62, 64.

Indeed divine power fashioned this helper not from similar or even from the same material. But as a more specific motivation for charity and friendship, this power created a woman from the very substance of the man. In a beautiful way, then, from the side of the first human a second was produced, so that nature might teach that all are equal or, as it were, collateral, and that among human beings—and this is a property of friendship—there exists neither superior nor inferior.[12]

There is no hierarchy in friendship. This may be another reason why friendship between the sexes is less likely in some environments that hold to female subordination in all cross-gender relationships. God's design was to produce women not only as sexual partners, haven-makers, and baby mamas to men, but also as friends to walk side by side with them.

One Friendship Doesn't Diminish Another (or Your Marriage)

Part of the beauty of friendship is that one friend can't possibly be adequate to share every discovery and experience with us. Having another lover would dishonor and diminish a marriage, but additional friends actually enhance the friendships that we already have. God has fashioned friendship in such a way that we can learn different facets about one friend from another.[13]

For example, my elder Dave Myers has a shared interest with me in friendship between the sexes, since his roles as a Christian counselor and a church elder deal with relationships.

12. Aelred, 66.
13. See Lewis, *The Four Loves*, 61.

We had many fruitful conversations on this topic as he read my manuscript and offered his insights. But my husband's friendship with Dave through their service in the church shows a different side of Dave to me. Additionally, we look up to Dave and his wife, Dawn, for encouragement and advice in parenting, as all their kids are grown. My friendship with his wife has taught me more about Dave's history and faithfulness. And, through his friendship with someone else at the church, I've learned that Dave is quite the jokester. Dave's many friends, and his exclusive relationship with his wife, boost my own friendship with him because they enhance his many qualities. I get to know more of Dave through other friends. Likewise, his and Dawn's many friends do not take away from their marriage but enrich it.

At the same time, we have a greater natural affection toward some brothers and sisters in God's household than toward others. While Scripture directs us to act in loving service toward all our siblings, we enjoy investing extra time with some of them, sharing joys, struggles, interests, and counsel more deeply. Some we will hold as closer friends. This isn't something to feel guilty about; Jesus himself had closer relationships with certain men and women than with others. It's impossible to be "close" with everyone, so enjoying deeper friendship with a few brothers and sisters is a gift. And these closer sibling relationships should benefit our godly marriages, not the reverse.

This is not only a warning for male-female relationships. I have seen numerous situations in which a husband is out with the guys so much that his wife is feeling neglected, or a husband is hurt by his wife's excitement for talking and hanging out with her best friend, while she lacks interest in him. Friends and siblings should never undermine a marriage unless abuse, addiction, or adultery calls for advocates to step in.

This is especially true with male-female relationships. I would never want another wife to feel threatened by my friendship with her husband. I would never want to step into their exclusive inner circle—not just physically, but emotionally as well. My aim for my brothers in Christ is that my friendship with them would encourage them to love their wives even more, and I expect the same from my brothers with whom I invest my own time in friendship. Friendship is not exclusive like marriage is, so there is no need to behave as if it were. Marriage is exclusive, and therefore we should care for it in that way.

Exclusivity in a marriage relationship does not mean that our spouses will fulfill all our relationship needs. While Matt and I have a lot in common and enjoy doing many things together, there are areas in which we are not as compatible, and we are both happy that we have numerous other people in our lives, both single and married, with whom we can still grow and can share those separate interests. Or sometimes I need the kind of conversation that I can get only with another sister, as wonderful as my husband is to talk to. While my husband is the only one I look to for romantic affection, it is unfair of me to look to him alone to fulfill all my social, emotional, and intellectual needs. We need good friends. That's why God has given us brothers and sisters as well.

Matt and I share most of our friends in common. I am thankful that my sisters and brothers in Christ spur Matt on in his love for me—whether through razzing him, encouraging him, or praising him. That's what siblings do! They look at us not as singles but as two people joined together in the covenant of marriage. Likewise, we honor our marriage by speaking well of each other to our friends. We want to build each other up to our siblings, and our siblings reciprocate the respect we have for each other. Matt and I do a good bit of socializing in groups and sometimes double-dating. We also open our home to friends often. So our brothers and sisters are familiar with more than just whichever one of us they may feel closer to; they are familiar with our marriage dynamic as well.

Friendship welcomes others into our circle who share our convictions. This is particularly special in the context of spiritual friendship, as Lewis points out, highlighting the joy of adding others into friendship while we all reflect Christ in different ways. "In this, Friendship exhibits a glorious 'nearness by resemblance' to Heaven itself where the very multitude of the blessed (which no man can number) increases the fruition which each has of God."[14] Additional friends do not diminish our existing friendships. Rather, we get to know more of Christ through our various Christian friends.

The Cost of Friendship

From what I've said, friendship sounds great! So why are we so cautious about it? One reason we are so cautious about friendship is because it costs us something. In his great essay "Friendship and Its Discontents,"[15] Alan Jacobs contrasts Jean-Jacques Rousseau's idea of friendship with Samuel Johnson's. Both men wrote letters, only six years apart, regarding whether a friendship each one had could be repaired after an offense against him. Johnson speaks of how his love for his friend covers the offense, and he assures his friend that he too will work to "repair the fault"[16] for the sake of the friendship. But Rousseau highlights the limits that a friendship has, saying,

14. Lewis, 62.
15. Alan Jacobs, *A Visit to Vanity Fair: Moral Essays on the Present Age* (Grand Rapids: Brazos Press, 2001), 75–78.
16. Jacobs, 76.

"I wish my friends to be my friends, and not my masters; to advise me without claiming to control me; to enjoy all kinds of rights over my heart, none over my freedom."[17]

But is what Rousseau describes really friendship? Consider how different his language is from Aelred's. Rousseau sounds pretty self-absorbed, does he not? Friendship can't work this way. Jacobs describes Rousseau as

> a kind of anorexic: having consistently refused the nourishment of genuine friendship, fearing some violation of the sleek purity of the imperial self, he lies upon the deathbed congratulating himself for having avoided unhealthy eating. Rousseau's self-deception is immense: he believes someone can have a claim upon his "heart" without infringing upon his freedom. What can this mean? Any form of human connection compromises one's freedom by bringing another's needs, and often another's suffering, into one's own life; that is the price to be paid for such attachment. Of course, not everyone is willing to pay that price: witness the Buddhist doctrine of nonattachment.[18]

Rousseau's notion of friendship sounds an awful lot like the view of those in the church who want to impose restrictions on friendship between the sexes. We don't look at ourselves as servants to our friends; instead, we look at them as threats to our imperial selves. Does this view of friendship between the sexes resemble the Buddhist doctrine of nonattachment more than the Christian doctrine of shared communion with the triune God? Do we take pride in being unstained by the thought of inappropriate interaction to the point that we cut

17. Jacobs, 76.
18. Jacobs, 77–78.

ourselves off from our call to love one another and therefore starve to death as a community? Is this how we attain holiness?

One way this is evidenced is when boundaries between men and women are used for "maintaining a high public reputation," in the words of a commenter on my blog—"If a well-known Christian man is seen in public alone with 'another woman' tongues will wag."[19] This attitude treats women the same way that the religious characters treated the dying man in the parable of the good Samaritan in Luke 10:25–37, in their efforts not to get polluted by him. Harsh boundaries pretend that "fornication is like the flu, and you accidentally catch it if you happen to be close to a woman."[20] Or maybe the Christian's reputation or image is polluted. Either way, Jesus calls us to be like the Samaritan, who cared for another human being in need.

This is how Christ loved us. This is how we should love one another. Pastor Sam Powell writes, "Take up your cross with him; despise the shame. . . . 'Let this mind be in you, that was also in Christ Jesus.' Perhaps it is time that we start thinking about love, rather than reputation."[21] The church should model this to the outside community. But too often, in an effort to maintain a pristine reputation, not only are some church leaders impoverishing themselves of genuine friendship, they are also impoverishing the church with their leadership model. We are Christians, not Buddhists.

The friendship that I described in this chapter does come with a cost. Johnson recognized this cost in his letters and

19. Craig Shier, December 2017, comment on Aimee Byrd, "Why Saying 'She's Just a Friend' is an Insult," *Housewife Theologian* (blog), *Mortification of Spin*, December 7, 2017, http://www.alliancenet.org/mos/housewife-theologian/why-saying-shes-just-a-friend-is-an-insult#.WsuY79PwaCf.

20. Sam Powell, "Billy Graham Rule Follow-up," *My Only Comfort* (blog), April 26, 2017, https://myonlycomfort.com/2017/04/26/billy-graham-rule-followup/.

21. See Powell.

looked at it as an investment. We have seen important considerations in the previous chapters regarding friendship between the sexes. Friendship requires rooted identity, mission, holistic value, purity, maturity, and growth. This is costly. Our Savior thought of the cost of being a friend to us, one that we could never afford, and warned us to count the cost before becoming his disciples. We aren't expected to pay what Christ did. But he did what we were unable to do so that we could take up his cross and follow in his path. Because of his sacrifice, I am able to have this mind-set about my friendships: "You and I are here, and I hope that Christ is between us as a third. . . . Gratefully let us welcome the place, the time, and the leisure."[22]

"Representation and Solidarity Matter"[23]

The Christian has great dignity and responsibility as an image bearer who is saved by grace through faith in Jesus Christ. The true God is so radically different from all false gods. He is outgoing and life-giving. And we are graciously called to participate in the Father's great love for his Son through his Spirit. He has taken rebellious, sinful creatures and brought us back into goodness.

> In Scripture we are presented with a radical portrait of divine generosity, with humanity given special place of privilege to embody and extend divine goodness and grace. This portrayal also has a radical democratizing effect, which cuts against ethnic, social, economic, and other differences that so separate humanity from one another. . . .

22. Aelred, *Friendship*, 55.
23. Kelly M. Kapic, "Anthropology," from *Christian Dogmatics: Reformed Theology for the Church Catholic*, ed. Michael Allen and Scott R. Swain (Grand Rapids: Baker Academic, 2016), 187.

Accordingly, humans were created to live not as isolated, autonomous individuals but in community with one another and in life-giving connection with the material world as the environment for communion with God.[24]

We see this demonstrated in the life of Jesus Christ here on earth, and we experience it now as his Spirit applies his work to us and empowers us to live in communion with God and our neighbors. Is this what we are representing to the world about Christ's church?

Even creation is tied up in God's message of salvation. In the creation story, God made man and woman to reign over the earth, and it was very good. He gave Adam and Eve a cultural mandate, saying, "Let Us make man in Our image, according to Our likeness; and let them rule over the fish of the sea and over the birds of the sky and over the cattle and over all the earth, and over every creeping thing that creeps on the earth" (Gen. 1:26). From the beginning we were made to serve God together in our labors on the earth. When man sinned, the earth was also put in bondage. When Christ returns, all those who are united in him will be given resurrected bodies, and there will be in a sense a resurrected earth—a new heavens and a new earth. And so even creation groans for that great day of Christ's return, when there will be a "revealing of the sons of God" (Rom. 8:19) and "the creation itself also will be set free from its slavery to corruption into the freedom of the glory of the children of God" (v. 21). Then we will reign with Christ in the new heavens and the new earth (see 1 Cor. 6:3; 2 Tim. 2:12).

We are made for community with one another, as *all* those who are united to Christ will be coheirs with him. Amazingly, we participate in this reign even now in connection with the

---

24. Kapic, 188.

world he has given us as we wait for that great day of consummation. We are so united to Christ that Paul tells us we have already been raised up and seated with him in the heavenly places (see Eph. 2:6). His church is given a new commission to spread his spiritual kingdom to the ends of the earth through the means of grace he has instituted (see Matt. 28:18–19). We don't want to reduce any of this message to the watching world!

Christians, this is who we are. We are God's people. We were created for joyful communion with him and one another. The Father has shared his love for the Son with us, through his Spirit. All mankind has dignity, as we are created in God's image. Do we represent this in the way we relate to others? Christians are called to exemplify God's love for mankind in Christ. And what a great love it is! "The faithful love of God was so great that he restored the true relationship with his mankind again in Jesus Christ, the true and genuine man."[25] We point one another to the incarnate Christ, and in doing this we are imitators of God. And even now we enjoy fellowship together in his household as sacred siblings. Let's encourage and exhort one another to be rightly ordered toward God, with all our faculties, and not to demote one another in our friendships. These relationships will benefit us as we are sent out into the world to be good neighbors to all creation.

Resurrecting the Friend Zone

"He's/she's just a friend."

Because we live in such a romanticized and sexualized age, in which every meaningful relationship with the other sex is expected to make its way to the bedroom, we often react by

---

25. From the confession of the Church of Toraja, Indonesia, quoted in Kapic, 189.

minimizing friendship. We set marriage up as the ultimate relationship in which all our commitment, passion, and intimacy is shared and invested. And, with the word *just*, we deny the gift of friendship and instead suggest that it does not call us to the worthy practices and commitments mentioned above.[26] What a rebellious expression of ingratitude—and what a demeaning way to describe our friends. It reveals the modern notion that friendship "is something quite marginal; not a main course in life's banquet; a diversion; something that fills up the chinks of one's time."[27]

God is full of grace, giving his people what they do not deserve and could never dream of. We aren't entitled to his affection and all that comes with it—he chose us in Christ. He doesn't just invite us in; he makes us part of the family. He does this by revealing the truth of who we are and who he is. And our Lord doesn't shirk from commitment; he makes covenantal promises and faithfully carries them through all the way. I'm not *"just* a daughter."

Let's be grateful for the friendships we have been given and the esteem of carrying out those responsibilities. Friendship is not a downgrade from erotic love. Unlike our marriages, friendship will last to the new heavens and the new earth. I would never call Matt *"just* my husband." I would never say that Luke, Brooke, Eli, and Brody are *"just* my brothers and sister." Likewise, it's a great honor to be called a friend. Friendship is something we value, so we promote one another's holiness as we pursue virtue together side by side.

---

26. While I can't endorse all of this book's teaching about friendship between the sexes, I appreciate Dan Brennan introducing this idea of being "just friends" in his book, *Sacred Unions, Sacred Passions: Engaging the Mystery of Friendship Between Men and Women* (Elgin, IL: Faith Dance Publishing, 2010), 107.

27. Lewis, *The Four Loves*, 58.

Discussion Questions

1. Consider your social media friend lists. Do you think that this kind of technological interaction has shaped your ideas about what friendship entails? Has it cheapened your view of friendship? How many of your social media friends would you say are genuine?

2. What are the longest-lasting friendships you have? What qualities do you think have helped them to endure so long? Who are your most unlikely friends? What brought you together?

3. What do you learn about Christ through your different friendships? How do you think you reflect Christ in them?

7

We've Overlooked Our Biblical Status as Brothers and Sisters

As I've blogged on the topic of friendship between the sexes, I've received a lot of pushback—usually from Christians. But at least I can say that the accusations haven't reached this level:

> Now as the world grows more wicked, your abominable shrines are sprouting up throughout the whole world. This entire impious confederacy should be rooted out and destroyed! You know one another by secret marks and insignia. You love one another almost before you know one another. Yours is a religion of lust. You promiscuously call one another brothers and sisters. You apparently do this so that your debaucheries will take on the flavor of incest.[1]

---

1. Mark Felix narrates these accusations in his apologetic work *Octavius*, published 150–210 A.D., available in Justin Martyr and Mark Felix, *We Don't Speak Great Things—We Live Them! A Modern English Rendition of Mark Felix's* Octavius *from the Translation of Robert Ernest Wallis and The First Apology of Justin Martyr from the Translation of Marcus Dods* (Tyler, TX: Scroll Publishing, 1989), 31.

This captures the Roman argument against Christianity in the early days of the church. Christians met in secret because they were being killed for professing their faith. The Romans heard of their love feasts, which included wine, brother-sister language, and holy kisses, and, well, tongues wagged.

> Your banquets are also well known and are spoken about everywhere. On a solemn day, all of you assemble together at the feast, along with your children, sisters, and mothers. People of every sex and age are present. After much feasting, when the group is boisterous and when incestuous lust has grown hot with drunkenness. . . . nature takes its course in the dark.[2]

The rumors spread because of the brotherly and sisterly love the Christians had for one another. The early church wasn't uptight about appearances. They didn't respond to the accusations by distancing themselves from one another. They lived according to their proper identity in Christ and their joint mission.

Siblings as Metaphor

When I started to look at how men and women are created to relate to one another in God's household in both today's world and the new heavens and the new earth, I saw language of brotherhood and sisterhood all over the place. Sure, we all know it's in Scripture. The church is also described as Christ's bride and as living stones that make up a building, with Christ as the cornerstone. But sibling language saturates God's Word in the New Testament even more than these other metaphors do—much more.

2. Martyr and Felix, 32.

Wayne O. McCready writes that "the amount of language emphasizing close personal ties, brotherly and sisterly love, greetings with a holy kiss, concern for the well-being of community members, and so on—not only reinforced a sense of community, but it underscored the internal cohesion that distinguished the assemblies of early Christians."[3] God's people are set apart in a special solidarity that is noticeable to the watching world.

Reidar Aasgaard, professor of intellectual history at the University of Oslo, points out that Paul uses sibling language to refer to Christians far more frequently than he uses any other term. Examining Paul's epistles to the Romans, 1 and 2 Corinthians, Galatians, Philippians, 1 Thessalonians, and Philemon, Aasgaard finds that Paul uses the Greek root referring to siblings more than a hundred times. In contrast, he uses the words *holy* and *church* fewer than fifty times each and words such as *called* and *body of Christ* only a handful of times.[4] This is a significant distinction! If this is Paul's favored way to address and describe his fellow Christians, then we should examine what he is communicating about us with this language.

Scripture often employs metaphors to use something we already know well in order to describe a symbolic resemblance, but not a literal reality. For example, when Jesus says he is the door (see John 10:7), we know that he isn't actually a piece of wood with a knob and hinges. The illustration of a door teaches us that Jesus is the only way to salvation. Similarly, Aasgaard believes that Paul calls us brothers and sisters in

---

3. Wayne O. McCready, *"Ekklesia and Voluntary Associations,"* in John S. Kloppenborg and Stephen G. Wilson, eds., *Voluntary Associations in the Graeco-Roman World* (London: Routledge, 1996), 63.

4. See Reidar Aasgaard, *'My Beloved Brothers and Sisters!' Christian Siblingship in Paul* (New York: T&T Clark, 2004), 3.

order to to teach us something about our relationships, even though we are not biologically related.[5]

Aasgaard asserts that Paul draws on what his readers knew about siblingship, one of the most powerful ancient social institutions, to show Christians how we are to relate to one another. Paul uses an ethical reality that was familiar to all, even though he teaches some novel applications of siblingship along with using it as a metaphor within a Christian context. He draws from the Jewish, Greek-Hellenistic, and Roman cultural traditions that his readers could relate to at that time,[6] so we will need to see what those involved.

Ancient Siblingship

One thing that surprised me, as I looked into these cultural contexts myself, was the size of the average household in ancient times. I had always assumed that without sophisticated birth control everyone had huge families like Jacob, with his twelve sons, or Job, with his seven sons and three daughters. But Aasgaard shows us a different picture. Due to early mortality rates as well as abortion, abandonment, and contraception if the household had enough sons, only two out of five children in ancient households would grow to adulthood. At ten years of age, a child might have about two living siblings; by age thirty-five, the average numbers drop to 1.5 living siblings.[7]

Add to that the fact that, by age twenty, only 50 percent of adults had living fathers and 60 percent had living mothers, and you will quickly realize just how valuable siblings were to one another. Emotional bonds between siblings often grow closer

5. See Aasgaard, 3.
6. Aasgaard, 35.
7. Aasgaard, 38. The author does say that Jewish families are suspected to have been a bit larger, but that there is no conclusive evidence to support this.

as they suffer through adversity together. And the household in those times needed to remain strong, as the family unit was the center of social contact, emotional life, religious traditions, education, justice issues, and economic production.[8] Siblings who survived their childhood and early adulthood years usually had "the most lasting of all family relationships."[9] While deaths changed the head of the household and shook up the siblings' responsibilities, the relationships between surviving siblings were an anchor to their family history and identity.

When Paul addresses fellow Christians as siblings, he emphasizes the strong emotional bond that he wants us to have. By using the metaphor of natural siblings in ancient households, he draws on the common knowledge that Christians should honor one another in this valued relationship, promote unity, and live in harmony, which was "a fundamental condition for a successful family life."[10]

In the book *The Ancient Church as Family*, Joseph Hellerman describes how this language in the New Testament teaches that God's people ought to have the same sibling solidarity and exclusive allegiance as a biological family.[11] And he notes that we immediately see the practical outworking of this in the communal life of the early church.[12] Luke sets the scene in Acts. As the early Christians share their goods with one another, they "[practice] fundamental Mediterranean kin group norms, including the 'obligation to be certain that the needs of everyone in the group are met.'"[13]

---

8. See Keith R. Bradley, *Discovering the Roman Family: Studies in Roman Social History* (New York: Oxford University Press, 1991), 8–9; Aasgaard, *Brothers and Sisters*, 45–48.

9. Aasgaard, *Brothers and Sisters*, 40.

10. Aasgaard, 54.

11. See Joseph H. Hellerman, *The Ancient Church as Family* (Minneapolis: Fortress Press, 2001), 18–25, 64.

12. See Hellerman, 21–22.

13. Hellerman, 22, quoting Scott Bartchy, "Community of Goods in Acts:

These ideals became more focused between the first century BC and the first century AD, as smaller households of immediate family members became prominent over the larger *familia*, in which extended family, freedmen, and slaves lived together.[14] The smaller household model fostered more gender balance than the strictly patriarchal *familia* model. People traced their family lines through both the mother and the father, rather than exclusively through the men.[15] This can be seen in Matthew's genealogy of Jesus, which includes Tamar, Rahab, Ruth, and Bathsheba (see Matt. 1:3, 5–6).

Most of the material written specifically on sibling relationships in ancient times comes from the Romans, but their writings are likely representative of Greek and Jewish household culture as well.[16] Sibling relationships throughout ancient Mediterranean cultures have common themes. The differing rights and obligations of brotherhood and sisterhood were more fluid than hard-and-fast rules. Brothers valued their sisters as much as they would another brother. Brothers had an obligation to protect their sisters, and their sisters' honor was as important to them as their own. If the father died early, brothers were to help to support their unmarried sisters. Even after a sister married, brothers were to take her side in any marital conflict. Yet even though brothers were expected to take on these paternal responsibilities toward their sisters, the relationship was different from a father-daughter one: "A sister could expect, and virtually seems to have had, a greater freedom and autonomy in the eyes of brothers than of fathers."[17]

Likewise, sisters cared deeply for their brothers. Sisterhood

---

Idealization or Social Reality?" in *The Future of Early Christianity: Essays in Honor of Helmut Koester* (Minneapolis: Fortress Press, 1991), 313.

14. See Aasgaard, *Brothers and Sisters*, 60.

15. Aasgaard, 41.

16. Aasgaard, 62. The following six paragraphs paraphrase his findings.

17. Aasgaard, 63.

allowed them to practice the responsibilities associated with being a wife and mother. Sisters nurtured household relationships, acting as arbitrators between brothers or the father and a brother during a conflict. Sisters also sometimes functioned as family representatives in the public sphere.

We don't have a lot of details on sister-sister relationships, as daughters were often the victims of abortive practices and abandonment, and men authored most of the sources available to us. But sisterhood was upheld as the idealized relationship in some of the literature of the time. It appears to have been an emotionally close relationship, in which sisters bore many of the same obligations to each other as between sisters and brothers.

Much more is available to us on fraternal relationships and obligations. "[Brothers] were representatives of the family towards the outside world, and were obligated to ensure that property was kept within the family . . . to protect the family against outsiders, and to defend the family's name and honour. Brothers were also expected to further each other's interest in public life."[18] A close bond between brothers promoted harmony in the household. But this harmony was often threatened by the competitive nature and emotional detachment that sprung from brothers' positioning in the family and their vying for inheritance, affection, and approval.

Many conclude that the brother-sister relationship was fairly egalitarian; but, while there is a lot of truth to that, this is too simplistic a label. First of all, we don't want to read our own social and cultural perspectives into the ancient culture. Ancient people just didn't think about relationships that way. Birth order and gender determined certain obligations that carried authority in different spheres, whether private or public. Yet these hierarchies "appear to have been shifting, complex,

18. Aasgaard, 67.

and fluid, in an interplay between factors such as age, gender, social status, and personal abilities."[19]

The idea of family didn't have the same romantic connotations that it has today, and households were not thought of as private havens. "The value Romans put on personal or familial privacy was in fact very low, and for them the house was multifunctional, a place of constant social, economic, and sometimes political intercourse, not simply a place of habitation."[20] Marriages were arranged from the outside, not because two people "fell in love," so harmony was their most important virtue.[21] Add to that the mixed families that arose due to death or divorce, and we get a picture of how siblings needed to work together and value their solidarity. Siblings were expected to love and serve one another, tolerating differences, compensating for weaknesses, and building on strengths in order to promote unity and harmony within the household.

Sibling love was praised during ancient times, with authors, historians, and philosophers such as Hierocles, Musonius Rufus, Valerius Maximus, Josephus, Philo, and the Qumran all writing on the topic.[22] They expected siblings to have a natural affection toward one another that bore fruit in their actions. Aasgaard devotes a whole chapter to Plutarch's essay "On Brotherly Love"[23]—a valuable complete text on sibling relationships in antiquity. Many of the themes I have mentioned play out in his treatise, highlighting how sibling love is distinguished from all other loves throughout a lifetime.[24]

So, when Paul calls his readers brothers and sisters, he draws on their knowledge of a special love, along with its

19. Aasgaard, 76.
20. Bradley, *Discovering the Roman Family*, 8–9.
21. See Bradley, 6–8.
22. See Aasgaard, *Brothers and Sisters*, 71–72.
23. See Aasgaard, chap. 6.
24. See Aasgaard, 105.

obligations, responsibilities, and pursuit of unity and harmony in diversity.

Our Spiritual Reality

Siblingship is not just a metaphor, however. Paul looks at us as siblings, and we are to look at one another as siblings, because our siblingship is a spiritual reality. Our siblingship is a status. This status even takes precedence over our biological sibling relationships.

We begin to see this in an exchange that takes place in Matthew 12. Jesus is teaching, surrounded by crowds, when he gets interrupted. "Someone said to Him, 'Behold, Your mother and Your brothers are standing outside seeking to speak to You'" (Matt. 12:47). Family deserves special attention, right? Even if Jesus is really busy, we expect him to say something like, "Tell them I will be there when I can." Instead, Jesus' reaction seems harsh.

> Jesus answered the one who was telling Him and said, "Who is My mother and who are My brothers?" And stretching out His hand toward His disciples, He said, "Behold My mother and My brothers! For whoever does the will of My Father who is in heaven, he is My brother and sister and mother." (Matt. 12:48–50)

We see elsewhere in Scripture that Jesus cares deeply for his birth family and that we should care for ours as well (see Ex. 20:12; Prov. 1:8–9; John 19:26–27; Eph. 6:1–4; 1 Tim. 5:8). But when Mary tries to use her position as biological mother to interrupt his teaching, Jesus points out that we aren't to look at him merely based on his fleshly genealogy. "This passage . . . informs us, that every one who is regenerated by the

Spirit, and gives himself up entirely to God for true justification, is thus admitted into the closest union with Christ, and
becomes one with him,"[25] writes theologian John Calvin. "He
admits all his disciples and all believers to the same honourable
rank, as if they were his nearest relatives, or rather he places
them in the room of his *mother and brethren.*"[26] This is something to behold! By faith, we are new creations with exclusive
family ties to Christ. We have an unremitting advocate who
is now seated at the right hand of the Father (see Ps. 110:1, 5;
Rom. 8:34; Heb. 7:25). He has already paved the way for us.

So what does this mean for us now as brothers and sisters
in Christ? We need to be careful not to impose our own social
understandings on spiritual realities but rather to pay attention to what God's Word teaches us when we use them. We
can't take all the things that we know about brotherhood in
our culture and apply them to Christ. But this metaphor is
used in Scripture for a reason—when we become believers,
we experience a change in status so that we have the blessing
of calling Christ our brother, and he warmly responds to this
truth. You see, when Christians are called brothers and sisters,
it's not merely a metaphor. Our union with Christ makes us
supernatural siblings.

As a son and sibling, Jesus has affection and rights and
obligations that he upholds. But he teaches us that, as new
creations, we have another sibling relationship. We don't get
to choose our brothers and sisters; they are assigned to us. And
we have rights and obligations to uphold with our spiritual
siblings that sometimes conflict with those of our biological
siblings. As this conflict is made apparent in the life of Jesus, we

25. John Calvin, *Commentary on a Harmony of the Evangelists, Matthew, Mark, and
Luke*, vol. 2, trans. William Pringle, Calvin's Commentaries 16 (repr., Grand Rapids:
Baker, 2003), 91.
26. Calvin, 90.

see both the priority he gave to the spiritual relationship when it competed with his natural family ties, as well as the proper love he gave to his biological siblings. We see this dilemma to some extent in the lives of his disciples as well.

Before his resurrection, Jesus' natural brothers do not believe him (see John 7:5). They have grown up with him, witnessing firsthand a man who never sins, and they have seen many of his miracles and works. Yet just after Jesus chooses his twelve disciples, his brothers exclaim, "He has lost His senses" (Mark 3:21). They think their brother has gone crazy! When Jesus returns to his hometown and teaches in the synagogue on the Sabbath, the murmurings begin: "'Is not this the carpenter, the son of Mary, and brother of James and Joses and Judas and Simon? Are not His sisters here with us?' And they took offense at Him" (Mark 6:3).

This is a real, painful tension. His own brothers do not understand who he is. Jesus knows about family rejection as well as renunciation from the people he grew up around. But he finds comfort in the reality of his spiritual family, which was growing. We can rejoice that, after his resurrection, Jesus' brothers were brought to faith. I would like to believe that his whole natural household was. James and Jude each wrote a book in the Bible, and James was also the leader of the Jerusalem council (see Acts 15).

Some other natural siblings embrace Christ as his disciples. Brothers Peter and Andrew and brothers James and John respond in solidarity when Jesus calls them to discipleship. They leave their belongings and obligations behind in order to follow the Christ (see Matt. 4:18–22). But walking away from one life to another competes with their natural family ties.[27] When the mother of James and John makes the special request

27. See Aasgaard, *Brothers and Sisters*, 68.

to Jesus for her sons to have prominence in the new kingdom (see Matt. 20:20–28), Jesus sets her straight about things she does not yet understand. Clearly there is much she still doesn't get about Christ's kingdom, but she is also promoting natural family relationships over spiritual brotherhood. Jesus insists on solidarity with the spiritual family.

Some suffer loss in their natural families when they embrace the family of God. Peter testifies to this. Jesus' response gives us a new reality, for which we can be grateful:

> Peter began to say to Him, "Behold, we have left everything and followed You." Jesus said, "Truly I say to you, there is no one who has left house or brothers or sisters or mother or father or children or farms, for My sake and for the gospel's sake, but that he will receive a hundred times as much now in the present age, houses and brothers and sisters and mothers and children and farms, along with persecutions; and in the age to come, eternal life." (Mark 10:28–30)

Jesus knows the pain of conflict with unbelieving family members. And, though he calls us to solidarity with our spiritual family over and above our natural, biological families, he promises to bless us richly in that supernatural family.

Today we think that abandonment or adultery in marriage is the worst betrayal. "Exactly the opposite is the case for Mediterranean antiquity. Treachery in its most extreme, despised and, therefore, engrossing form is not the breakup of a marriage but strife among blood brothers."[28] Giving up loyalty to one's biological brothers and sisters is an ultimate sacrifice, but Jesus promises a hundred times as much family now in the present age . . . and in the age to come. Our

28. Hellerman, *The Ancient Church as Family*, 39.

surrogate family in God's household is superior even to our natural families. And it doesn't form in the future; it begins now.

A Religion of Incestuous Lust, or Supernatural Siblings?

We are supernaturally adopted siblings in Christ. "Adoption changes status. It also changes hearts. It changes everything."[29] This is why Christians are directly addressed in Scripture as siblings so many times—ninety-two times, to be exact.[30] Aasgaard notes that this affectionate form of address is used more frequently by Paul in the practical sections of his letters, where the theology he has just taught is applied to Christian behavior and relationships.[31] The Romans recognized this special affection and let their imaginations run wild. Nevertheless, Paul uses it to appeal to Christians to remember who they are and how they are related to one another. He also uses this direct address when he shares secret knowledge. For example, "Now I do not want you to be unaware, brothers and sisters . . ." (1 Cor. 10:1 csb), or "We do not want you to be uninformed, brothers and sisters . . ." (1 Thess. 4:13 csb).[32] This method of address makes us lean in, paying extra attention as we receive exclusive teaching. Something special is revealed to us that changes the way we think and live.

Christians have a high standard that comes with our status as siblings. As antiquity shows us, siblingship comes with rights and obligations and honor and affection among members of

29. David B. Garner, *Sons in the Son: The Riches and Reach of Adoption in Christ* (Phillipsburg, NJ: P&R, 2016), 72.
30. See both the appendices in Aasgaard, *Brothers and Sisters*, 313–14, for a chart of all instances.
31. See Aasgaard, 273–74.
32. See Aasgaard, 278.

a family. But siblings in Christ have an even higher calling. Since we are siblings in Christ, we ought to pray (see 1 Thess. 5:25), we ought to stand firm (see 1 Cor. 15:58), we ought to turn from idolatry (see 1 Cor. 10:14), and we especially ought to rejoice in the Lord (see Phil. 3:1).[33]

Let's return to the Roman accusation that Christianity is a religion of lust. What should our witness be to the outside world? We should model sibling solidarity, in which siblings honor one another, have affection for one another, live in harmony, promote familial unity, mature together, and treasure our special sibling relationship. Ancient siblings lived by this ideal, and they were tied by only a narrow bloodline. They cherished their special relationship as a way to get them through life. But ours is the bloodline of Christ, which carries with it victory over sin, grace that abounds, transformative sanctification, and life everlasting. We are not just living for a legacy here on earth. We are new creations with a holy eternal destiny.

We have not only a supernatural sibling status, but a supernatural love. Paul tells us in Romans to "love one another deeply as brothers and sisters." Rather than merely honoring one another, we are to "outdo one another in showing honor" (Rom. 12:10 csb).

When instead we regard one another as temptations, as means merely of gratifying sexual desires, or as threats to our image, and we do not regard one another honorably as brothers and sisters, we are not loving deeply. And what, then, does the world see about God's plan for his household? For the new earth? Are we suggesting that we have a cruel God who says that he made us to be brothers and sisters in Christ when we can't control our sexual impulses enough to be friends?

---

33. See Aasgaard, 280.

Remembering Who We Are

Most of us fall somewhere in between this extreme and our biblical call to be sisters and brothers. Many of us would like to have richer friendships but struggle to show the special affection that the Spirit deeply desires to cultivate in our relationships with one another: to love one another honorably and therefore freely. It's easy for us to think we are playing it safe when we adopt rigid rules that keep us from showing affection for one another. But, when we do, we are forgetting our sibling status.

Christians often get burned when they rightly order their affections with the other sex, as the mere appearance of closeness can lead to accusations of bad motives. And sometimes there is a real battle going on as we fight through temptations and work them out before the Lord. It's easy to confuse legitimate desires for intimacy, closeness, and meaningfulness in our friendships with illegitimate romantic notions—even if only in our thoughts. This is the case both within our relationships and as observers of others.

Loving another person deeply does not come naturally. Yet, at the moment of temptation, this is exactly what the Spirit calls us to do. We are part of a supernatural family, and we depend on the Spirit for supernatural help as we are called to a supernatural love. Do we seek self-indulgence and reduction, or do we seek sacrifice and honor? Rather than assuming that friendship is impossible and walking away—or, worse yet, plowing forward to indulge or seduce—we will acknowledge and confess any wrongful ruling passions to the Lord and will ask him for wisdom and power in order to deeply care for our siblings in Christ.[34]

---

34. I am indebted to Dave Myers, who gave me most of the words in this paragraph in editing.

And this is what we hope unbelievers will notice about us. We would like them to see holy relationships, right?

What Natural Siblings Teach Us

We can begin to think of how this will look practically in our lives when we look at biological siblings. There are some differences in how we relate to brothers versus how we relate to sisters. Some of them have to do with personality, and some have to do with gender. These differences are difficult to describe in a universal way, but our experiences help us to grasp the nuances.

Growing up, I did rely on a certain protectiveness from my brother Luke, even as I myself am protective of all my siblings (especially, since I am the eldest). I feel a lot of freedom around my brothers to be myself. I know that they will never threaten me. Sisters don't have to worry whether our brothers are misinterpreting our affection for them. We should know that they honor us. What a special relationship!

But there is a different bond between brothers and, likewise, between sisters as well. There is something to a fraternal bond that I just don't know because I lack that experience. But I have twin seventeen-year-old brothers who have a great camaraderie that is unique to males. One observation about this special bond is that it again provides a freedom for males to have affection for one another without ever having to worry about it being romantic. Brothers help to fulfill the God-given need that males have for male affection in the appropriate way. And brothers are often passionate both in the way that they fight and in the speed at which they can get over it and make up.

And although I loved growing up with my brother for the first three years we had alone together, I also prayed for a sister, and God delivered her to me when I was six years old. I knew I was lacking something, because sisters too share a special bond. I once read that a sister is like a human diary, and I thought that was a good description. Sisters can bear their souls to one another. The term *sisterhood* is often used to describe the power that sisters create when they work together for a united purpose—they can be unstoppable. Sisters are also passionate when fighting—sometimes I think even more so than brothers. While brothers tend to be more physical with one another, sisters can hurt each other far worse with their words and actions.

Our siblingships are usually the longest-lasting relationships in our lives. So it is fitting that we share the status of siblings with God's people, because our siblingship will never end in death. And, even as there are many nuances that are hard to pin down regarding how gender affects our relationships, siblingship showcases how our sexes are complementary to each other.

So how does God get us there? As we move into how we *can* be friends, the language and practices of siblingship become imperative to how we are encouraged to relate to one another in Scripture. We will see how this identity as sacred siblings shapes our affections, rights, and responsibilities to one another, as well as consider steps we can take to cultivate holy, affectionate friendships in God's household and beyond.

Discussion Questions

1. If an unbeliever were to observe the relationships and culture within your church, what do you think he would say? Would he see anything that is set apart or different from his own world?

2. What kind of rights do you have in God's household as a supernatural sibling? What obligation does that bring?

3. Have you had to make any sacrifices as a spiritual sibling? What have these sacrifices taught you about your status in God's household? Is there anyone in your church who has left behind a whole biological family's comforts on Sunday morning in order to go to church? What could you do to model the truths of Matthew 12:48–50 today?

PART 2

How Do We Live as
Sacred Siblings?

8

Find Our Sibling Identity
in Our Elder Brother

Technological advancements have given rise to a lucrative business that helps people to trace their ancestry. We want to know our roots. We value not only this generation of our family but also the many before. We want to know our family story—how we got where we are today. My beloved grandma passed away recently, and at her funeral service I was full of wonder to see older women from my grandfather's side of the family walking around with the same eyes as me. It made me want to get to know them. Even though these distant family members are basically strangers to me, I would love the chance to grab some lunch and learn about them.

There are many different types of family relationships, but siblingship has always been one of the most valued. Aristotle considered it equal to the relationship between a parent and child, ahead of the marriage relationship, and Sirach gave it the highest honor, over friendship and marriage.[1] Joseph Hellerman describes siblingship in ancient Mediterranean families as the relationship with the "deepest sense of emotional bonding and support"—one in which brothers and sisters formed "the tightest unit of loyalty and affection."[2] In Sophocles' fifth-century play *Antigone*, the title character laments that the death of her brother is worse than the death of her husband. If her husband dies, she can at least remarry and still bear children; but she will never gain another brother.[3] This is a powerful thing to say. It drives home the point that siblings are irreplaceable!

When I was younger, I often wished I had an older brother to watch out for me and have my back. I am the eldest sibling, and part of me wanted to have someone else to pave the way before me and be there as an advocate anytime I needed them. But I have been blessed with a close relationship with my younger siblings. My brothers and sister and I address one another with our sibling titles as a term of affection. So when I see Luke, I'll smile, nod, and say, "brother," and he usually responds with a smile, nod, hug, and "seester." It shows that we are happy to see each other and that we have a unique position in each other's lives.

It's one thing to be told that we have a sibling status with fellow Christians. But how do we really understand and feel that bond? In the last chapter I introduced the wonderful truth that Christ is our Elder Brother. What can we glean from this title? What does Christ fulfill for us as our Elder Brother?

---

1. See Reidar Aasgaard, *'My Beloved Brothers and Sisters!' Christian Siblingship in Paul* (New York: T&T Clark, 2004), 61, referencing Aristotle's *Nichomachean Ethics*, 8.12.1–6.

2. Joseph H. Hellerman, *The Ancient Church as Family* (Minneapolis: Fortress Press, 2001), 36.

3. See Aasgaard, *Brothers and Sisters*, 64–65.

Our Keeper

It's interesting that the first relational devastation we see after the fall is not between husband and wife but between brothers. The ideal of unity, harmony, and sibling love is torn apart when Cain fails miserably as Abel's older brother. As I reread that story in preparation for writing this section, I was shocked to see how many times the word *brother* is used in it—seven times in Genesis 4:2–11! Abel is described over and over again as Cain's brother, to remind us of the affection and responsibility that Cain was to have toward Abel.

Unlike with Adam and Eve, God doesn't ask Cain where he is after Abel's murder. But he does pursue him with the question "Where is Abel your brother?" And Cain responds with the now infamous "I do not know. Am I my brother's keeper?" (Gen. 4:9). This is a brazen response. Does Cain actually think that God doesn't know where Abel is? Or is he passing the blame onto God himself? He certainly abdicates his blessing and responsibility as a brother.

So *keeper* is the first word the Bible uses to describe the brotherly relationship, even though it's used in a contemptuous way. When Cain wittingly replies to God, "Am I my brother's keeper?" he unwittingly reveals so much about siblingship. His retort reveals that, while playing dumb and denying this basic truth, he actually does know what it means to be a sibling. We too know that the answer is "Yes! Yes, you are your brother's keeper!" But what does that mean, exactly?

We're only into the fourth chapter of Genesis, but that same word has already been used to describe Adam's vocation in the garden: "Then the LORD God took the man and put him into the garden of Eden to cultivate it and keep it" (Gen. 2:15). To *keep* means to guard and protect—even in a priestly sense, as Adam and Eve served in a holy temple-garden before the fall. But they did not fulfill this mandate. "As priest[s] and guardians of the garden, Adam and Eve should have driven out the serpent; instead it drives them out."[4] Similarly, Cain is driven out from his home and doomed to wander as a vagrant (see Gen. 4:12). No one would want Cain for an older brother! The world's first brother cared only about himself.

As our Elder Brother, Christ is our keeper. Psalm 121 is all about that.

> Behold, He who *keeps* Israel
> Will neither slumber nor sleep.
>
> The LORD is your *keeper*;
> The LORD is your shade on your right hand.
> The sun will not smite you by day,
> Nor the moon by night.
> The LORD will protect [or *keep*] you from all evil;
> He will *keep* your soul.
> The LORD will guard [or *keep*] your going out and your
>   coming in
> From this time forth and forever. (Ps. 121:4–8)

The best-intentioned biological brothers could not possibly fulfill the vocation of keeping one another to this degree. But Jesus claims that position—the keeper of Israel, the keeper of his church; he has kept us in the Father's name and hasn't lost even one whom the Father has given him (see John 17:12). Psalm 121 shows us that Jesus can do this because he is the keeper of our souls. Charles Spurgeon remarks, "Soul-keeping is the soul of keeping. If the soul can be kept, all is

---

4. Bruce K. Waltke with Cathi J. Fredricks, *Genesis: A Commentary* (Grand Rapids: Zondervan, 2001), 87.

kept."[5] While Cain resented his brotherly responsibility to care for Abel, Jesus graciously assumes this office, "fulfilling it in person."[6]

He does this through suffering. To be our Elder Brother, Jesus assumed flesh and blood so that he could truly guard and preserve us from eternal death by living the life that we could not live and dying the death that we all deserved. Cain took Abel's life because he was jealous of the Father's affection for him. Jesus gave his own life so that we could share in the Father's name and in eternal communion with him. This is the beautiful story of brotherhood.

> For in bringing many sons and daughters to glory, it was entirely appropriate that God—for whom and through whom all things exist—should make the source of their salvation perfect through sufferings. For the one who sanctifies and those who are sanctified all have one Father. That is why Jesus is not ashamed to call them brothers and sisters, saying:
>
> I will proclaim your name to my brothers and sisters;
>
> I will sing hymns to you in the congregation.
>
> Again, I will trust in him. And again, Here I am with the children God gave me.
>
> Now since the children have flesh and blood in common, Jesus also shared in these, so that through his death he might destroy the one holding the power of death—that is,

---

5. Charles Spurgeon, *The Treasury of David* (1869; repr., Peabody, MA: Hendrickson, 1988), 3:16.
6. Spurgeon, 3:15.

the devil—and free those who were held in slavery all their lives by the fear of death. (Heb. 2:10–15 csb)

Jesus, the keeper of our souls, is the ultimate priest who brings us into communion with the Father through the Spirit. Why is it fitting for Jesus Christ to be our Elder Brother? How does he bring many sons and daughters to glory? Or, more specifically, how do we get to be called *sons*? This is a very important point of our salvation, which is connected to Jesus' role as our Elder Brother. It is also a key to our question about relationships between the sexes.

"Sons in the Son"[7]

Cain may have been the first older brother, but he wasn't the first created son. That honor goes to "Adam, the son of God" (Luke 3:38). As God's son, Adam had a "filial destiny" to fulfill God's covenant by righteously expanding the garden-temple to the ends of the earth, earning covenantal inheritance and blessing for himself and all his progeny.[8] But Adam was not the obedient son.

Sonship language is also used for the nation of Israel, which is referred to as the firstborn son (see Ex. 4:22; Jer. 31:9; Hos. 11:1). But Israel was not the obedient son.

Praise God that he sent a second Adam to do what the first Adam could not (see Rom. 5:12–18; 1 Cor. 15:20–49)! Even before Adam, God had a plan to adopt his sons and daughters in the eternal Son of God.

David Garner's fabulous book *Sons in the Son* teaches that Paul uses the term *adoption* in Scripture to explain that our

---

7. See David B. Garner, *Sons in the Son: The Riches and Reach of Adoption in Christ* (Phillipsburg, NJ: P&R, 2016).
8. See Garner, 45.

union with Christ is familial, bearing all the benefits of sonship. We see this in Ephesians:

> Blessed be the God and Father of our Lord Jesus Christ, who has blessed us with every spiritual blessing in the heavenly places in Christ, just as He chose us in Him before the foundation of the world, that we would be holy and blameless before Him. In love He predestined us to adoption as sons through Jesus Christ to Himself, according to the kind intention of His will, to the praise of the glory of His grace, which He freely bestowed on us in the Beloved. (Eph. 1:3–6)

"For Paul, the entirety of our redemption—from the mind of God before creation itself until its eschatological completion in our bodily resurrection—is expressed by *filial* reality, *filial* identity, and a *filially framed* union."[9] The doctrine of adoption has a legal aspect, just like any earthly adoption. But Paul isn't talking about merely a legal act but a new eschatological reality in the Son. "The believer is *adopted* and then lives forever as an *adopted son*. For Paul, redeemed sonship permanently remains adoptive sonship."[10] We have been made sons in the Son.

Back the truck up, Aimee. I thought we were talking about brothers *and* sisters, sons *and* daughters? Why all this talk about our being sons? Shouldn't we use more gender-inclusive language? Not here, Garner says—because Paul is very selective with the Greek word (*huiothesia*) that we render in English as *adoption*. This word has the word *son* (*huios*) in it, so that "adoption is, literally, *son placing*."[11] Why does this matter? Because it highlights that the gospel is fulfilled in Christ the Son. "*Huiothesia* occasions Spirit-facilitated gracious *placement*

9. Garner, 34.
10. Garner, 50.
11. Garner, 51.

in and perfect *solidarity with* the *huios.*"[12] The Son of God is male, and to use a gender-neutral term would lose the force of this connection between the Son of God and the redeemed sons of God. All the redeemed, male and female, make up the bride of Christ and are sons in the Son.

Heirs of God

Paul further develops what adoption accomplishes for the believer in some other passages, which Garner breaks down for us. I will comment briefly on a few of these.

In Galatians, Paul shows that sonship develops from the old covenant, in which believers had only a taste of what was brought to maturity in the new covenant. Now, through the Spirit, sons in the Son experience what those under the old covenant had hoped for—to join with the "exalted *messianic* Son, so that the believing sons of this age enjoy the privileges of mature sonship as attained by their Elder Brother."[13] We are heirs through God!

> When the fullness of the time came, God sent forth His Son, born of a woman, born under the Law, so that He might redeem those who were under the Law, that we might receive the adoption as sons. Because you are sons, God has sent forth the Spirit of His Son into our hearts, crying, "Abba! Father!" Therefore you are no longer a slave, but a son; and if a son, then an heir through God. (Gal. 4:4–7)

By faith and through the power of his Spirit, we share in this sonship, which includes the intimacy of a family, access to the

---

12. Garner, 51.
13. Garner, 97.

Father, and the full inheritance of the resurrected Christ. And by this power we can be obedient sons as we are transformed into the likeness of the Obedient Son.

> You have not received a spirit of slavery leading to fear again, but you have received a spirit of adoption as sons by which we cry out, "Abba! Father!" The Spirit Himself testifies with our spirit that we are children of God, and if children, heirs also, heirs of God and fellow heirs with Christ, if indeed we suffer with Him so that we may also be glorified with Him. (Rom. 8:15–17)

Garner points out that from the repetitive use of the word *Spirit* throughout Romans 8, we see the eschatological thrust to Paul's argument.[14] The Spirit applies to us the work of the resurrected Christ who is seated at the right hand of the Father. In this new age, Christ's kingdom has been inaugurated; the future breaks into the present as the Spirit leads and empowers us, as new creations, to live according to who we are! And as his Holy Spirit leads us, we are called to live lives of faith and obedience. In this age, we can expect these to involve suffering, just as our Elder Brother suffered in obedience before us. The tension between this age and the age to come is a place of struggle, even as we grow in our filial affection as sons in the Son. Yet again we see the real benefit of redemptive adoption—we can call out to the holy Father as our own. Is there a sweeter communion than this?

> We know that the whole creation groans and suffers the pains of childbirth together until now. And not only this, but also we ourselves, having the first fruits of the Spirit,

14. See Garner, 104.

even we ourselves groan within ourselves, waiting eagerly for our adoption as sons, the redemption of our body. (Rom. 8:22–23)

As with our justification, sanctification, and resurrection as new creations, our adoption also has an "already and not yet" component that makes us groan. Even creation groans with us for the great day of "the revealing of the sons of God" (Rom. 8:19). We see that the redemption of our bodies, our resurrection, is connected to our Elder Brother's. Because of who he is—the eternal Son, incarnate and resurrected in victory as the adopted Son[15]—we already have the firstfruits of his Spirit. We know that our end is to be resurrected in his image. And we also know that we are far from this now. How we groan and cry out to the Father as we eagerly await the consummation and completion of our adoption.

Siblings in God's House

As we look at what Scripture teaches about Jesus as *our* Elder Brother, it is important for us to note again the blessing of siblingship. He is *our* keeper. *We* are sons in the Son. *We* are heirs of God. Cain, the first earthly brother, despised brotherhood. He wanted God's affection his way. He didn't rejoice in the Lord's regard for his brother's offering. But we are siblings in Christ.

One thing that siblings have in common is a household. After writing about our adoption in Christ and all the blessings that come from the Father in him, Paul tells us, "He made known to us the mystery of His will, according to His kind intention which He purposed in Him with a view to an

---

15. See Garner, chap. 7, "Jesus Christ, the Son of God Adopted."

administration suitable to the fullness of the times, that is, the summing up of all things in Christ, things in the heavens and things on the earth" (Eph. 1:9–10). What is this mystery? What new thing has been revealed? We know that Jesus is preparing a new heavens and a new earth for us to inhabit together in our resurrected bodies, but even now he is summing up all things, in heaven and on earth, into his household.[16] The fall of man brought chaos to God's household, the place where he dwelt with his people. But, as our Elder Brother, Christ is managing and administrating an eternal dwelling place that we are brought into by our union with him. Then all will be set right in heaven and earth. Garner explains, "'The summing up of all things in Christ means the unifying of the cosmos or its direction toward a common goal,' the goal of sweet cosmic harmony, a harmony displayed by the Spirit-wrought unity and community of the sons of God in Christ (2:11–22; 4:1–32)."[17] Our sonship places us in a new family in God's household.

When I heard as a kid about Christ's preparing a new home for us, I wondered what was taking so long. He has the power to do it whenever he wants. I envisioned him rearranging the furniture, as it were, of rivers, jewels, and mountains. But in this summing up of all things, Jesus takes his time in rearranging our hearts and our wills and transforming them into his very likeness. Part of this is rightly ordering our love and affection for one another. We get dress rehearsals for this new household every Sunday in our local churches, don't we? And he has instituted a means of grace by which we are being sanctified, growing and maturing together as sacred siblings, as we share in his mission.

16. See G. K. Beale and Benjamin L. Gladd, *Hidden But Now Revealed: A Biblical Theology of Mystery* (Downers Grove, IL: IVP Academic, 2014), 148.

17. Garner, *Sons in the Son*, 69–70, quoting from Andrew T. Lincoln, *Ephesians*, Word Biblical Commentary 42 (Dallas: Word, 1990), 33.

We have our personal households, many of which include brothers and sisters, and we have our spiritual household, the church, which is full of our brothers and sisters in Christ. We serve together, focusing on a common goal: to be summed up in the household of God, wholly set apart for his purposes, as we reign with him in the new cosmos.[18] That is our goal! How does it shape our interactions and relationships now? We should be maturing in personal holiness and love for one another. That unity in community should be a part of our experience in our own households, as we are summed up into the household of God.

Our Ultimate Blessing

When I think about the sibling harmony and the Spirit-wrought community that Christ is summing us up in, I have to wonder about the fracturing I see in relationships between brothers and sisters in the church now. While we assent to the knowledge that we are part of God's church, we don't think enough about how the church is the household of God. It reminds me of another sibling relationship in Scripture in which the older brother did not apprehend the blessing of his inheritance. He took his identity for granted, and his desires were misplaced. This is a danger for us as well. We also need to be careful to uphold the spiritual status of our siblings. In our continuous battle with sin, are we treating one another like Esau, who was consumed by his temptation because he was too sensuous to see the blessing that lay ahead? Is that all that we are to one another—stumbling blocks? No, we know this isn't true. Our Elder Brother showed us that he is the

18. See Aimee Byrd, *No Little Women: Equipping All Women in the Household of God* (Phillipsburg, NJ: P&R, 2016), 79. See the entire third chapter for more on household mission, management, and the stewardship of God in our local churches.

blessing that lies ahead, while also showing us how to love our brothers and sisters. Are we embracing any false teaching about who we are?

You see, to live by the Billy Crystal rule is to say something very different about what our blessing is and who we are. For Crystal's character Harry Burns, women are a means to his biggest blessing: sex. That was all he could think about when interacting with women. Burns gives the advice of many earthly big brothers, doesn't he? (Maybe I should say, many eighteen-year-old earthly brothers!) Unfortunately, many men and women do not grow out of this adolescent thinking. Burns was so sensuous that he could not see the real blessing that lay ahead in godly friendships, and so he was insatiable. Every woman became a means for his consumption.

Singles, take some time to think about this. If you don't know how to love well in friendships, you will never be satisfied with a spouse. Why? Because sex never satisfies when you view it as a means to self-gratification. Those who think that way will always look at their partner reductively as a means for their own pleasure. And if you look at your spouse that way, you will look at others that way as well. Yes, sex is a blessing in marriage—an exclusive sharing of oneself with one's spouse in the most vulnerable way. It is a joining of two into one. But it was never designed to be our ultimate blessing. And we can enjoy it much more when we know this truth.

Sex does not make us whole. Our Elder Brother is the most satisfied and fulfilled person who ever walked this earth, and he never married or had sex. He had deep friendships and intimate fellowship in all purity, because he had already experienced the most satisfying communion of all. And he is outgoing in sharing the blessed communion of the triune God with his siblings. "In Jesus, God actualizes his call to us to enter communion with him through the Son and by the

Spirit."[19] We become like God in the most blissful way—we get to share in his love for the Son through the Spirit! In that love we find true fulfillment and satisfaction.

My original longing for an older biological brother recognized a real need. We all need the true Elder Brother. Unlike Esau, our Elder Brother obtained the blessing so that we can be blessings to one another in him. Since I have come to learn about identity in my ultimate blessing, Jesus Christ, I have found that I have many older spiritual brothers in his household. Brothers and sisters, let's behold the grace of God together and spur one another in fellowship with the Son.

Discussion Questions

1. What is particularly special about biological sibling relationships? How do these factors transfer, and how are they even enhanced, in our spiritual brother and sister relationships?
2. How does Jesus contrast with some other older brothers in Scripture, such as Cain, Esau, or the brother in the Lost Son parable (see Luke 15:11–32)? How does Jesus fulfill all that we need in an older brother?
3. What is our filial responsibility to one another with Jesus as our Elder Brother?

19. Kelly M. Kapic, "Anthropology," from *Christian Dogmatics: Reformed Theology for the Church Catholic*, ed. Michael Allen and Scott R. Swain (Grand Rapids: Baker Academic, 2016), 167.

9

Cultivate a Church Environment
That Supports Sacred Siblingship

As far back as the beginning of time, we can see the importance of households. The first household was like nothing we have on this side of the resurrection. God placed Adam and Eve in a garden where everything was holy, consecrated to the Lord. Therefore their household was also a temple—a place for God's presence. The man and woman were to subdue their household unto the Lord, expanding "the garden and God's sacred presence on earth."[1] They failed in this vocation. After the fall, Adam and Eve were cast out of the sacred paradise.

The fallen world is not holy; we share our cultural tasks *in common* with unbelievers. Gardens are not holy, coffee cups are not holy, and soccer is not holy. They are common—part of our secular life. But Jesus Christ, the second Adam, uses the means of his spiritual rule in the church to expand God's

---

1. G. K. Beale, "The Temple and the Church's Mission" (lecture, Christ Reformed Church, Anaheim, CA, March 30, 2007), available online at http://links.christ reformed.org/realaudio/20070330a.mp3.

presence throughout the whole earth. He consecrates a people to himself, and his people make up God's holy household—his temple. As we serve him in our different cultural contexts, we long for the day when everything will be holy again. Hey, even our coffee cups will be holy: "In that day there will be inscribed on the bells of the horses, 'HOLY TO THE LORD.' And the cooking pots in the LORD's house will be like the bowls before the altar. Every cooking pot in Jerusalem and in Judah will be holy to the LORD of hosts. . . . And there will no longer be a Canaanite in the house of the LORD of hosts in that day" (Zech. 14:20–21). Jesus Christ is preparing a holy garden-city where we will dwell eternally with him. Meanwhile he calls a people to himself and transforms us into his likeness. His church is a holy household.

Harmony in Households

In chapter 7, we saw that household structures in antiquity were different from the ones in contemporary American culture. Siblings in antiquity had different freedoms, rights, and obligations within their households, and different levels of authority were set in place by factors such as birth order, gender, giftedness, and marital status. A woman's authority was limited to the private sphere of the home, whereas a man's authority extended to the public sphere of society. Women did not share the same social status as men. In an honor-shame society, women upheld family harmony and honor by subordinating themselves to the men in these social structures.[2]

Scripture does not overlook the plight of women in ancient culture—it exposes it and shows us faithful, brave women

2. See Keith R. Bradley, *Discovering the Roman Family: Studies in Roman Social History* (New York: Oxford University Press, 1991), 6–9; Reidar Aasgaard, *'My Beloved Brothers and Sisters!' Christian Siblingship in Paul* (New York: T&T Clark, 2004), 52.

who took initiative for the advancement of God's kingdom.[3] Today, women rightfully participate alongside men in society, receiving distinctive authority based on skill, opportunity, and other factors. But our personal household dynamics still affect a society's success.

The ancient family household was considered a microcosm of society, so its unity and harmony were vital to the public sphere. In a sense, a society is only as good as the households that make it up. If personal households are in chaos, then the greater society will suffer. This means that good household management is vital to social order. Although household codes have changed in our contemporary culture, some things will always be the same. Households function well when their members work in unity and harmony to carry out their mission and to witness to those outside. Good household management doesn't just happen organically. Someone needs to sacrificially serve the family in order to help it achieve its purpose. A household manager bears the weight of the family's responsibility to maintain order in carrying out its mission.

What is the purpose of a household? Adam and Eve were given the mandate to expand their household and God's sacred presence throughout the earth, building and creating from what God had given them. As household manager, Adam was a federal representative of mankind. He represented all of us with his obedience or rebellion, and Eve was his ally, joined to him in marriage so that they functioned in unity and harmony.[4]

The fall fractured their household, but God, in his grace, did not change his mission of pursuing us for holy communion

---

3. A few examples are Tamar, the midwives in Exodus, Rahab, Ruth, Esther, Deborah, Abigail, Jael, the Cannanite woman who approaches Jesus for healing for her daughter, the woman at the well, Martha and Mary, Priscilla, and Phoebe.

4. See Aimee Byrd, *No Little Women: Equipping All Women in the Household of God* (Phillipsburg, NJ: P&R, 2016), 71.

with himself and one another. Every created being in every personal household is commanded to love our God with all our hearts, souls, and minds and to love our neighbors as ourselves (see Matt. 22:37–39). We are able to do this only through our Elder Brother, Jesus Christ.

What is the mandate of God's household, the church? Jesus gives this commission: "Go . . . and make disciples of all the nations, baptizing them in the name of the Father and the Son and the Holy Spirit, teaching them to observe all that I commanded you; and lo, I am with you always, even to the end of the age" (Matt. 28:19–20). The church's mission is to spread the good news of salvation in Jesus Christ through the preached Word, discipleship, and administration of the sacraments.

The Gift of Household Managers

Let's pause in reflection for a moment. If our personal households are a microcosm of society, then unity and harmony in God's household should model the cosmos of the new heavens and the new earth. Even more so, God's household needs a good manager to carry out his mission.

And of course God graciously does not withhold that from us. Jesus Christ is *the* household manager who sums up all things by unifying his household in its mission: harmonious worshipful communion with the triune God for eternity in the new heavens and the new earth. And, as the greatest household manager, he does this with order and administration, not leaving us in chaos.

Through his Spirit, Christ has gifted all the members of his household to work in harmony toward his mission (see Rom. 12:3–8; 1 Cor. 12:4–18). When Jesus ascended, he gave the church gifts to carry out this mission (see Eph. 4:8). "He gave some, apostles; and some, prophets; and some, evangelists; and some, pastors and teachers; for the perfecting of the saints, for the work of the ministry, for the edifying of the body of Christ" (Eph. 4:11–12 KJV).[5] God gives us the officers of the church to promote our sanctification through the ministry of the Word and sacraments[6] "until we all attain to the unity of the faith, and of the knowledge of the Son of God" (Eph. 4:13). The ministry of the Word is prioritized so that God's household receives Christ and all his blessings before we gratefully serve in response. This ministry unifies and matures us in good doctrine, so that we can minister to one another according to its truths.

Throughout the New Testament, we see that Christ's kingdom is unlike the kingdoms of society. Christ, our King, does not micromanage us—he serves us! And he requires that those who represent him as leaders in the church also serve the rest of the household. The elders in our churches have a responsibility as our representatives for spiritual oversight, government, and discipline in God's household. They are heads who lead the household to carry out its mission. But headship in God's household should awe those in the world. This headship is

> accomplished thorough a reversal of the world's expectations of this duty, a reversal that is grounded in the significance of Christ's own saving actions and reflects the paradoxical values of the kingdom.
>
> In the world the life of the body revolves around the head, and its role in the unity of the body is particularly important. For example, Seneca describes the head, Caesar, as "the bond by which the commonwealth is united" (*Clem.*

---

5. For these verses, the King James Version gives a better translation of the Greek construction of the text (see Michael Horton, *The Christian Faith: A Systematic Theology for Pilgrims on the Way* [Grand Rapids: Zondervan, 2011], 887–88).

6. See Horton, 887–88.

1.4.1). For Paul, the head is also the source of unity, but only as the head acts in a manner that is very unheadlike, by not exerting power or privilege but rather doing the opposite.[7]

As heads of the church, elders are to exemplify shepherding care as they tend to our mission, "until we all reach unity in the faith and in the knowledge of God's Son, growing into maturity with a stature measured by Christ's fullness" (Eph. 4:13 CSB). They do this not by exploiting their rights to power but by laying aside their rights in loving service to God's people.

One Anothers

A lot of ink has been spilled on the scope of the authority of ordained leaders and who is and isn't qualified for this headship role. These are important conversations. But there has been less talk about 97 percent of the church—the laity. What rights, obligations, and relationships do we find between brothers and sisters in God's household?

We do talk about special ways that we are called to service according to our spiritual gifts. Peter instructs us to be good stewards of our gifts in serving one another: "As each one has received a special gift, employ it in serving *one another* as good stewards of the manifold grace of God" (1 Peter 4:10). Sometimes I think that we fret about what our gifts are and how we can use them best, as if our spiritual gifts are the main way we edify the church and relate to our brothers and sisters. But, although each of us is uniquely gifted to serve God and our brothers and sisters, we share a lot of *one another* exhortations in common—almost sixty.

7. Michelle Lee-Barnewall, *Neither Complementarian Nor Egalitarian: A Kingdom Corrective to the Evangelical Gender Debate* (Grand Rapids: Baker Academic, 2016), 162; see also Ephesians 5:21–33.

The first of these exhortations in the Bible teaches us a lot about kingdom reversal. Rather than exploiting all the privileges of the honored position of headship, in Christ's kingdom the head "fulfills his duty through the application of kingdom values rather than exercising his worldly rights."[8] So our head, Jesus Christ, washes feet; and we are told to do the same. "If I then, the Lord and the Teacher, washed your feet, you also ought to wash *one another's* feet" (John 13:14).

We can categorize the rest of these *one anothers* like so:

Love One Another

> A new commandment I give to you, that you love *one another*, even as I have loved you, that you also love *one another*. By this all men will know that you are My disciples, if you have love for *one another*. (John 13:34–35) [That sounds pretty strong and convicting. But siblings can be hardheaded and quick to forget, so this same command is sprinkled through Scripture another twelve times: John 15:12, 17; Rom. 13:8; 1 Thess. 4:9; 1 Peter 3:8; 4:8; 1 John 3:11, 23; 4:7, 11, 12; and 2 John 5.]

> Love *one another* deeply as brothers and sisters. Outdo *one another* in showing honor. (Rom. 12:10 CSB)

> May the Lord cause you to increase and abound in love for *one another*, and for all people, just as we also do for you. (1 Thess. 3:12)

> For you were called to be free, brothers and sisters; only don't use this freedom as an opportunity for the flesh, but serve *one another* through love. (Gal. 5:13 CSB)

8. Lee-Barnewall, 162.

. . . So that there may be no division in the body, but that the members may have the same care for *one another*. (1 Cor. 12:25)

Live in Peace and Harmony with One Another

Be at peace with *one another*. (Mark 9:50)

Live in harmony with *one another*. Do not be proud; instead, associate with the humble. Do not be wise in your own estimation. (Rom. 12:16 CSB) [The NASB translates it, "Be of the same mind toward *one another* . . ."]

Therefore, let us no longer judge *one another*. Instead decide never to put a stumbling block or pitfall in the way of your brother or sister. (Rom. 14:13 CSB)

Therefore, accept *one another*, just as Christ also accepted us to the glory of God. (Rom. 15:7)

Teach, Admonish, and Instruct One Another

My brothers and sisters, I myself am convinced about you that you also are full of goodness, filled with all knowledge, and able to instruct *one another*. (Rom. 15:14 CSB)

Let the word of Christ richly dwell within you, with all wisdom teaching and admonishing *one another* with psalms and hymns and spiritual songs, singing with thankfulness in your hearts to God. (Col. 3:16)

. . . Speaking to *one another* in psalms and hymns and spiritual songs, singing and making melody with your heart to the Lord. (Eph. 5:19)

. . . Submitting to *one another* in the fear of Christ. (Eph. 5:21 CSB)

Greet and Welcome One Another

Greet *one another* with a holy kiss. (Rom. 16:16; 1 Cor. 16:20; 2 Cor. 13:12; see also 1 Peter 5:14)

Therefore, my brothers and sisters, when you come together to eat, welcome *one another*. (1 Cor. 11:33 CSB)

Be hospitable to *one another* without complaint. (1 Peter 4:9)

Don't Do to One Another . . .

But if you bite and devour *one another*, take care that you are not consumed by *one another*. (Gal. 5:15)

Let us not become boastful, challenging *one another*, envying *one another*. (Gal. 5:26)

Do not lie to *one another*. (Col. 3:9)

Don't criticize *one another*, brothers and sisters. Anyone who defames or judges a fellow believer defames and judges the law. If you judge the law, you are not a doer of the law but a judge. (James 4:11 CSB)

Brothers and sisters, do not complain about *one another*, so that you will not be judged. Look, the judge stands at the door! (James 5:9 CSB)

Bear with One Another

Bear *one another's* burdens. (Gal. 6:2)

. . . With all humility and gentleness, with patience, bearing with *one another* in love. (Eph. 4:2 CSB)

. . . Bearing with *one another*, and forgiving each other. (Col. 3:13)

Be kind and compassionate to *one another*, forgiving *one another*, just as God also forgave you in Christ. (Eph. 4:32 CSB)

Clothe yourselves with humility toward *one another*. (1 Peter 5:5)

Do nothing from selfishness or empty conceit, but with humility of mind regard *one another* as more important than yourselves. (Phil. 2:3)

Encourage One Another

Therefore comfort *one another* with these words. (1 Thess. 4:18)

Therefore encourage *one another* and build up one another. (1 Thess. 5:11)

But encourage *one another* day after day, as long as it is still called "Today," so that none of you will be hardened by the deceitfulness of sin. (Heb. 3:13)

And let us consider how to stimulate *one another* to love and good deeds, not forsaking our own assembling together, as is the habit of some, but encouraging *one another*; and all the more as you see the day drawing near. (Heb. 10:24–25)

Therefore, confess your sins to *one another*, and pray for *one another* so that you may be healed. (James 5:16)

God's people actively pursue deep, loving relationships. This doesn't mean that we ignore sin and enable it but that we serve a common mission, acknowledging that we are all growing toward sanctification together. We teach one another all the truths of the faith, and therefore we take responsibility to know these doctrines. We speak truth to one another in love, we work to advance one another in the faith, and we bear with one another as we stumble. We don't leave a struggling brother or sister alone to fight, but we encourage and exhort, helping one another to the end.

These exhortations form a household code that helps us to pursue holy intimacy between siblings by showing love in practical ways. Which ones convict you? I was recently having a conflict with someone I love and didn't know how to pray about it . . . until I providentially wrote this section and realized that I was not bearing with my sibling in Christ very well. I needed to pray and repent.

If you are a parent, perhaps this section sounds familiar. We use the same language to promote healthy, loving sibling relationships. Just as the heads of the church are called to sacrificial love, so are we. When our churches demonstrate this love, we show the world that we view one another as new creations headed for a glorious new household.

Corporate Challenges for Sisters in God's Household

I would like to get practical regarding corporate challenges for siblings in God's household today. And I am going to focus on churches that believe, as I do, that the Bible mandates that church and personal households have authorized men as their heads. Not all men in the church function as heads, but the churches I am addressing understand Scripture to uphold that the ordained office is for certain qualified men only. They also understand Scripture to teach that in marriage the husband is the head of the household.

The first challenge is the physical vulnerability of women. Everywhere in society, women are more vulnerable than men. Typically men are taller and have greater muscle mass, grip strength, and bone density. A typical man can easily overpower a typical woman. Therefore, women are more susceptible to bullying, control, and abuse. This makes us physically vulnerable. Everywhere. All women are aware of this—all the time.

A second challenge is that in a church with exclusive male governance, women will never fill the office of ruling or teaching elder. This leaves us vulnerable in multiple ways.

Who will speak for the women in the church during the session meetings?

Women are dependent on male leadership to represent them. Sure, women can technically come to a session meeting, as any layperson can. But women are very aware that if they begin showing up to session meetings without a personal invitation, they may be suspected of trying to usurp male authority.

Officers in the church, have you ever thought about personally inviting some women to your session meetings and carving out time in your agenda to ask them good questions? This would be a great way to gain insight into the needs of the sisters in your church. What are their challenges? What are their strengths? This will be invaluable to your preaching, your shepherding, your discipling, and your prayers. Women may not be ordained elders, but from the beginning of the church they have been integral allies to men.

This should be a consideration when you are vetting and training officers in the church. The church needs leaders who recognize and appreciate allies, who work and communicate well with women—not just other men. Are men rising to leadership positions who lack the character and maturity to assume them? Are they being properly equipped in what headship actually entails? Do they understand what authority looks like in Christ's kingdom? Leaders should be approachable, not intimidating. They should be trustworthy. And all members under their care should see that they are represented well.

Who will equip the women theologically?

When elders recognize theological acumen in men in the church, they get excited. These men are potential elders, so they will be invested in as such. Elders may train them as small group leaders, invest in personally discipling them, send them to conferences for further learning, or even help to support them through seminary.

What do elders do when they notice theological vigor and sharpness in a woman? Sometimes these women are affirmed as women's ministry teachers. Often they are not properly equipped by the church for the position and are left to themselves, vulnerable to every wind of doctrine lurking on Christian radio and marketed in the Christian bookstores.

Paul entrusted Phoebe to deliver his epistle to the Romans. Who do you think the Roman church asked when they had questions about areas in Paul's important letter to them?[9] Paul had to be confident that Phoebe was well equipped for this responsibility that he gave her. Priscilla was able to discern that Apollos had the right intentions but was missing a key element of the gospel (see Acts 18:18–28). She was well equipped, along with her husband, to serve as a necessary ally to Apollos in spreading the true gospel to many.

9. See Michael F. Bird, *Bourgeois Babes, Bossy Wives, and Bobby Haircuts* (Grand Rapids: Zondervan, 2012), 20–21.

Officers, which women in your church demonstrate gifts of leadership and theological acumen? How are these gifts being nurtured, challenged, and used in your church? How do you invest in the women in your church? How do women serve the whole church with these gifts?

Who will come alongside women who are oppressed and abused?

Since women are physically weaker than men, since many women in the church are dependent on their husbands' salaries, since everyone in the church is a sinner, since Satan hates the church, and since there are wolves in sheep's clothing, we can expect cases of abuse in every church. Whether abuse happens in a marriage, in another relationship, or within the leadership of the church, whom does an abused woman have to go to as an advocate? It is intimidating for a woman to face a session of male authority with intimate details of abuse. This too exposes her vulnerability.

A responsible confessional church will recognize and acknowledge this. If it does not, a church with exclusive male governance is more vulnerable to patriarchy, weak relationships, bad doctrine, enabling of abuse, and immature men and women. Elders should have a strong conviction that their sisters in Christ are every bit as valuable as their brothers are. Not only that, women are needed as necessary allies[10] in God's household. But women are vulnerable under exclusive male governance, so it will take a concerted effort by the leadership to equip, listen to, and provide a welcoming atmosphere and a place for spokeswomen representatives in their inner circle. That's what good leaders do.

10. See John McKinley, "Necessary Allies: God as *Ezer*, Woman as *Ezer*," lecture, Hilton Atlanta, November 17, 2015, mp3 download, 38:35, http://www.wordmp3 .com/details.aspx?id=20759.

I love everything about my Traverse except for the blind spot. It's a great car, but if I don't compensate for the blind spot by doing some extra surveillance and actually maneuvering my body to get the full picture of what's around me, someone could get hurt. Thankfully it's been only a trash can and a couple of parked cars in my driveway so far. . . . And, the thing is, sometimes the church can be a lot like my Traverse. Abuse can be a blind spot for many well-intended elders who value their sisters in the church. Why? Because they don't want to look at them as vulnerable. They see many strong women in their churches, as well as many good men who also value their sisters in the faith and many wonderful husbands who strive to love their wives as Christ loves his church. But, if we aren't aware of our blind spots, we endanger others. Recognizing potential abuse will help leaders to be preemptive against further disaster.

Loving and wise shepherding will get ahead of this issue. Officers, seek out a few mature, compassionate, and competent women in your church to invest in. Make it known to your church that if anyone is being hurt, they can safely come forward to the advocates you have appointed to guide them through the process. In addition, develop relationships with a few good counselors, inside or outside your church, whom you can recommend for them. Abuse needs to be reported, but the victim should never be left to fend for herself afterward. Loving siblings actively provide a way for the abused to come forward, sending the message to the church that God's household is full of sacred siblings who will be protected and properly cared for. Ignoring or covering up abuse should be unheard of in God's household. We should be there for our hurting brothers and sisters.

Maybe your church does one or all of these well. Strength is found in knowing our vulnerabilities; and, in confessional churches, this puts a greater responsibility on the men. But this is also an opportunity to build sibling relationships and better serve the body.

Identify and Avoid False Siblings in the Church[11]

There is another major threat to the harmony and unity of God's household: not everyone is who they say they are—even in the church. Some pretend to be siblings when in fact they are not. With all this talk of love and harmony in God's household, I must warn that on the great day of consummation and glorification, Christ will reveal imposters in our midst. Paul calls us to identify those who masquerade as brothers and sisters. They are not harmless. These frauds use our family name to exploit our filial blessings to their malicious ends.

In the book of Galatians, Paul talks about "false brethren . . . who had sneaked in to spy out our liberty which we have in Christ Jesus, in order to bring us into bondage" (2:4). These false brethren had slipped into the council meeting in Jerusalem, insisting that all God's people needed to be circumcised. Paul doesn't say that they made a mistake and need to be taught differently, or that for the sake of unity in the body we need to get along and tolerate their teaching. He doesn't refer to them as weaker siblings, as he does to those in 1 Corinthians 8 who have weak consciences. No, these guys were attacking first-order theological issues to try to change the gospel, and they were no brothers at all. Certain gospel liberties must be protected within the household of God. Paul, with the backing of the council of apostles, will not stand for any of his siblings being brought into bondage.

Later, when Paul defends his status as an apostle to the

---

11. See Aasgaard, *Brothers and Sisters*, 300–303.

Corinthian church, he lists all the tribulations he has suffered as a servant of Christ, including prison, beatings, lashes, stoning, and shipwreck. Then he describes the dangers of his travels: "dangers from rivers, dangers from robbers, dangers from my countrymen, dangers from the Gentiles, dangers in the city, dangers in the wilderness, dangers on the sea, dangers among false brethren" (2 Cor. 11:26). Isn't it interesting that Paul mentions false siblings right alongside shipwrecks and robbers?

Paul uses a similar expression when warning the Corinthian church to disassociate from immoral people in the church. He carefully distinguishes between immoral people *outside* the covenant community and those within who claim to be believers while living in sin. He tells the church "not to associate with any *so-called brother* if he is an immoral person, or covetous, or an idolater, or a reviler, or a drunkard, or a swindler—not even to eat with such a one" (1 Cor. 5:11). We are called to judge whether those within the church are living according to their profession of faith. They may not be real siblings. The church joyfully receives a repentant sinner, but anyone living in continuous, unrepentant sin is to be removed from God's household and familial blessings.

It may sound hurtful to be exclusive and say to someone outside the church, "You are not one of us. You are not a sister." But an outsider may potentially be brought into the family of faith. It is far worse to be called a false sibling. We are to evangelize outsiders. But Paul says that false siblings want to put us in bondage; they are dangerous and immoral, and we should avoid them.

Similarly, the writer to the Hebrews strongly warns those who have tasted the covenant blessings in the visible community of the church and then revealed that they were never of the faith:

For in the case of those who have once been enlightened and have tasted of the heavenly gift and have been made partakers of the Holy Spirit, and have tasted the good word of God and the powers of the age to come, and then have fallen away, it is impossible to renew them again to repentance, since they again crucify to themselves the Son of God and put Him to open shame. (Heb. 6:4–6)

These aren't Christians who somehow lost their salvation. They were never real brothers and sisters. It's heartbreaking to think of the blessings they have turned away from, thereby shaming the very person and work of Christ.

This is a sobering call for us all to look out for our brothers and sisters in Christ,

see[ing] to it that no one comes short of the grace of God; that no root of bitterness springing up causes trouble, and by it many be defiled; that there be no immoral or godless person like Esau, who sold his own birthright for a single meal. For you know that even afterwards, when he desired to inherit the blessing, he was rejected, for he found no place for repentance, though he sought it with tears. (Heb. 12:15–17)

Here again we see an ungodly older brother given as an example. Esau's hedonism revealed that he had no regard for spiritual blessing. There was no real repentance to be found in him, only self-pity. The "root of bitterness" refers to Deuteronomy 29:18, where the Israelites are warned to turn from the false teaching that turns men's and women's hearts away from the Lord. False teaching produces the poisonous fruit of apostasy.

These examples point out how imperative it is for

households to have good stewards who uphold order, discernment, unity, and harmony among their members. Jesus hasn't left us to figure all this out by ourselves, but instead, as our Elder Brother, the household manager, he gives the gifts of the ministry to his church. In our churches, we receive these gifts through the preaching of the Word and the sacraments.

Jesus gave his church a mission to spread the gospel and make disciples. He sent his Holy Spirit to carry out that mission. We aren't left alone to make disciples, grow in the faith, and discern false siblings in the church. We have the living Spirit of God powerfully working in us. And he will perfect his purposes for the church (see Phil. 1:6). The church is a microcosm of our future household in the new heavens and the new earth. Does your church culture reflect this reality?

Practices That Support Siblingship

Thriving communion produces thriving communities. The quality of our relationships in God's household and the way we advance God's mission together testify powerfully to the real fruit of the gospel.[12] Merely avoiding challenges doesn't create friendship or cultivate good sibling relationships. We have to invest in our relationships through active measures. Author Christine Pohl argues that Christians should aim to live *into* our church communities through shared practices.

> Biblical descriptions of the church as God's household, as the body of Christ, and as a new family of brothers and sisters leave many of us dissatisfied with church life that is defined by a weekly worship service and an occasional

---

12. See Christine D. Pohl, *Living into Community: Cultivating Practices That Sustain Us* (Grand Rapids: Eerdmans, 2012), 2.

committee meeting or mission project. . . . Communities in which we grow and flourish, however, last over time and are built by people who are faithful to one another and committed to a shared purpose.[13]

Pohl encourages us to pursue church family communities in which we are confident in God's grace, his faithfulness to the fruit of our salvation, our unified mission, and our love for one another. Then we are free to take the necessary risks that contribute to our growth in Christlikeness. The practices that we exercise together regularly underwrite this relational dynamic. They include "hospitality, making and keeping promises, truthfulness, gratitude, Sabbath-keeping, testimony, discernment, forgiveness, worship, healing, and many others."[14]

We rehearse these practices so regularly that we rarely notice them—until they are lacking. "In general, practices are most powerful when they are not noticed, when they are simply an expression of who we are and what we do."[15] Pohl's examples of important practices to exercise in Christian community are vital to a thriving community. They are practices that help us to promote holiness in one another.

In the next few chapters, we will take a closer look at how these shared practices are a vital part of Christian friendship and promote holiness in our relationships.

Discussion Questions

1. Are you an officer of the church? Does the leadership in your church reflect the kingdom reversals that Christ taught to his disciples, or does it hold on to the power

13. Pohl, 3–4.
14. Pohl, 5.
15. Pohl, 6.

structures of the world? How does this affect the way that you relate to the laywomen and laymen in your church?

2. Would you describe your church as harmonious? Are the sisters invested in as much as the brothers? How has this chapter helped you examine the culture in your church, and what might you do differently?

3. How do the "one another" commands in Scripture and the shared practices I listed—hospitality, making and keeping promises, truthfulness, gratitude, Sabbath-keeping, testimony, discernment, forgiveness, worship, healing, and many others—underwrite holy brother and sister relationships in the church? How do they help us to identify false siblings?

10

Promote One Another's Holiness

I just want you to be happy. Parents, siblings, and friends say this all the time. They say it with good intentions. But what do they mean? What makes someone happy?

Most of the time the word *happy* is used to describe how we feel. But happiness is an elusive goal if we gauge it by our feelings. It's circumstantial. When we evaluate relationships with the litmus test *Does So-and-So make me happy?* it's also pretty selfish. How often have you heard the excuse "He doesn't make me happy anymore" as the reason for a divorce? Or an affair? How many people chase happiness by clamoring for wealth? The thing is, sometimes we're happy and sometimes we're not. It's natural to want friends who make us happy. But what if happiness isn't what we think it is?

Jesus, our friend and Elder Brother, shares the secret of true happiness with us in his Sermon on the Mount. He opens with a number of sayings, called Beatitudes, that begin, "Blessed [or *happy*] are those . . ." Jesus' description of being blessed differs starkly from how most people would describe happiness. We often base happiness on favorable circumstances,

167

emotional highs, and immediate gratification. The Beatitudes focus on humility, holiness, and properly oriented emotions. Of course, as he lists these qualities, Jesus is describing himself. R.C. Sproul teaches that "[blessedness] is the supreme dimension of happiness. It's not just a passing fit of glee or delight, but it is something that penetrates into the deepest chamber of our souls by which the soul is overwhelmed by a sense of sweetness and delight and satisfaction and contentment that knows no bounds."[1] Sproul explains that those who are blessed bask in the unveiled glory of God's face. This is pure communion.

This pure communion, the "supreme hope of the Christian life," is called the *beatific vision*.[2] What is that? It is to see God as he is. Then "the fullest aspiration of our humanity will be made complete,"[3] and we will experience true happiness, true blessedness. God promises that "ultimate satisfaction" "will flood the human soul, when in our glorification . . . we will see him as he is."[4] This is much different and much more specific than the happiness we talk about today. The truth is that when we persevere for true happiness, we wrestle with real or threatened loss, which brings us to a place of deeper desire for and rest in Christ.[5]

But our God is a holy God, and we are still not glorified. In this age, although we have been declared holy and set apart as God's people, and although his Spirit tabernacles in us, we still battle sin until either death or Christ's return. We will not

---

1. R.C. Sproul, "The Beauty of Being Blessed by God," lecture, in "The Beatitudes" series, *Renewing Your Mind* (radio broadcast), Ligonier Ministries, August 11, 2014, available online at http://renewingyourmind.org/2014/08/11/the-beauty-of-being-blessed-by-god.

2. Sproul.

3. Sproul.

4. Sproul.

5. Thanks to my elder, Dave Myers, for this thoughtful insight.

see God as he is until we are made completely holy—that is, until our glorification. Although we are given many blessings, we long for this ultimate blessing.[6]

This means we can quit looking to our family, friends, lovers, health, and other circumstances in life for ultimate blessing. But we do want to help each other toward true happiness, don't we? Our relationships should promote one another's holiness, in preparation for the Great Day when we behold the beatific vision—true blessedness.

Practicing Gratitude

When Cain asks, "Am I my brother's keeper?" (Gen. 4:9), it's as if he is saying, "Abel is *just* my brother; that doesn't mean anything. What am I supposed to do, keep a prison watch over him?" His reply suggests that Abel is on his own. It shows no gratitude for the gift of having a sibling, no commitment to him, no common mission with him, no connection with him whatsoever. No love. His reply rebelliously rejects who he is as a sibling. But Cain isn't God, and he can't just declare the way things will be. He is a brother. And, therefore, he *is* his brother's keeper. Even murder does not change this truth. Likewise, the sacred sibling relationship that Christian brothers and sisters share is a gift that comes with responsibilities. As important and honorable as it is to keep one another, sacred siblings are called to do more than that. Christians have the great honor and responsibility of promoting one another's holiness.

Attempts to promote holiness won't go far without gratitude. Most of us know how to praise God and say that we give

6. An insightful question from Dave Myers: "What if we really got it that this longing—which we will always lack here in part—is behind so much disappointment that we misread?"

him all the glory. We know how to thank one another. We're pretty good at that. But something about gratitude is humbling. Practicing gratitude acknowledges that we are dependent receivers. This can be difficult for me to do. When it is, it's usually because receiving makes me feel indebted, and I don't like to be in that position.

Additionally, I often don't want the interruption in my life that a giver brings. Christine Pohl notes that busyness and ambitions hinder our capacity to pause and take notice of God's gifts.[7] We pack our schedules with good things. But then there isn't any more room left, or we're just plain fatigued. When things do go wrong, we don't have space in our schedules to accommodate it, "and we are unable to receive any gift that might come in the form of an interruption."[8]

Pohl also points out that we can easily miss "important but overlooked connections between Sabbath and gratitude."[9] Sunday interrupts us. As we busily serve in our vocations, we tend to fall into our default habit of building our own kingdoms. But in our Sabbath worship, the age to come breaks into this age that is wasting away. Sabbath worship reminds us that we are receivers.

Pohl writes, "Seneca wisely warned that 'one should never accept a gift if one would be ashamed to acknowledge the debt publicly' (Ben 2.23.1); a gift should be accepted only if the recipient is willing to 'invite the whole city to witness it.'"[10] Isn't this what we are summoned to do on Sunday? God calls us out from our workweek to accept, as a covenant community, his gifts of the preached Word and the sacraments. The

---

7. See Christine D. Pohl, *Living into Community: Cultivating Practices That Sustain Us* (Grand Rapids: Eerdmans, 2012), 30.
8. Pohl, 30.
9. Pohl, 30.
10. Pohl, 40.

whole city witnesses our leaving behind the common activities of life for the sake of sacred worship. Sabbath reminds us that we are to rest in Christ. It "is both a response of gratitude and a context for gratitude."[11] God forbid we would not respond by assembling together and receiving his gifts to us.

Tim Keller once talked about a woman who had been visiting his church for a short time. She approached him after a service, explaining that she had gone to church her whole life and had never before heard the message of grace that he preached. She wanted to know why. Keller turned the question back to her, asking why she thought this gospel message had not been preached. The woman's response was both simple and profound. She said that if this message of salvation by grace alone was true, then there was nothing that God could not ask her to do that she would not have to obey.[12]

We would like God to owe us for our goodness and accomplishments. This woman understood that receiving the gift of salvation establishes a new relationship. She was a new creation, and she owed her life to God. That is our joy as we see that he has given us himself.

Gratitude is a way of life for those who recognize our greatest gift of salvation and communion with the triune God. Sunday worship and Sabbath rest are a way of life for us that point to eternal communion with him. We receive this gift not individually but as a household, not neglecting to meet together (see Heb. 10:25).

Friendship is one of God's gifts. The strange part is that

11. Pohl, 57.
12. See Tim Keller, "Gospel Communication" (lecture given at "Smashing False Idols: Evangelism in a Post-secular Society," the 5th annual Evangelists Conference, London, October 9, 2007), available online at http://www.evangelists-conference.org.uk/2F014-02GospelCommunication.mp3.

many Christians today are afraid to publicly acknowledge before our fellow evangelicals any affection or friendship with the other sex, denying altogether this gift and the responsibilities that come with it. In the new heavens and the new earth, men won't be separated from women, we won't pour all our affection, intimacy, and passions into our spouses, and we will be too spiritually mature to pretend that we don't need the gift of siblinghood and friendship with the other sex. So it's imperative to practice appropriate ways to express our gratitude to both the Giver and one another now.

Friends and Advocates

If it were up to us, we would still be Jesus' enemies. And yet Jesus pursued us for holy friendship. The cost that he paid for friendship with those who were bent to hate him should make us wonder in awe. His saving work on the cross would make us fortunate to be even his servants. But he calls us friends—and not only that, he tells us what kind of friend he is:

> No longer do I call you slaves, for the slave does not know what his master is doing; but I have called you friends, for all things that I have heard from My Father I have made known to you. You did not choose Me but I chose you, and appointed you that you would go and bear fruit, and that your fruit would remain, so that whatever you ask of the Father in My name He may give to you. (John 15:15–16)

As our friend, Jesus reveals the Father's will to us. As our friend, he invites us into communion with the triune God. As our friend, he chose us. That's what friends do. And because Jesus is our friend, we become holy.

The Father reveals what holiness is, first in his law and then in his Son, Jesus Christ. In Christ he declares us to be holy. But not only that! We also bear the fruit of holiness. Jesus promotes our holiness. He has made known the Father's will for us, he has accomplished the work to make us holy, and he has sent his Spirit to apply that work to us. Right now he is at the right hand of the Father, interceding on our behalf as our unremitting advocate.

Growing up together, siblings often bicker and insult one another. Children are like this. But, even still, most siblings have an underlying code: I may be able to insult my brother, but no one else can! Siblings usually stand up for one another in public if one of them is dishonored. As we mature, we drop the bickering and insults and more fully embrace our position as advocates—as those who publicly promote our siblings' best interests. Mature siblings often still tease one another in fun—and this reveals that the relationship involves intimate knowledge of one another and a safe place for playfulness. Because siblings are advocates, they can lay down their defenses and relate in a more unpretentious manner.

The writer to the Hebrews tells us that because our Elder Brother is our advocate, we have confidence to enter into the holy presence of God in all purity (see Heb. 10:19–22). He even addresses us as siblings—"Therefore, *brothers and sisters . . .*" (v. 19 csb)—before exhorting us with three "let us" statements:

> *Let us* draw near with a sincere heart in full assurance of faith, having our hearts sprinkled clean from an evil conscience and our bodies washed with pure water. *Let us* hold fast the confession of our hope without wavering, for He who promised is faithful; and *let us* consider how to stimulate one another to love and good deeds, not forsaking our own assembling together, as is the habit of some, but

encouraging one another; and all the more as you see the day drawing near. (vv. 22–25)

Because our Elder Brother intercedes as our eternal High Priest, we can draw near to God. Because our Elder Brother keeps his promises, we can hold fast to our confession of hope that Jesus is Lord in his person and in his work. Because Jesus is Lord, we will not remain in the sinful patterns of the flesh. We are exhorted not to waiver from persevering in the truth. And because we are God's people, siblings in Christ, we are to promote one another's holiness, which includes rousing one another to active, godly love, assembling with our siblings to publicly worship our God, and encouraging one another in godly living. These are practices of sacred siblings. They seem pretty ordinary, but, when exercised by those with God's Holy Sprit, they lead to extraordinary results.

The two words *let us* are easy to skip over, but they indicate that these are not individualistic practices and that they don't produce merely individualistic results. These are exhortations to the household of God—to siblings. Personal holiness is facilitated by sibling advocacy, and so the whole household grows in Christlikeness.

Practicing Encouragement

We are good self-talkers, and we can build a dialogue with ourselves that convinces us that we deserve some time away from the body. *No one will notice if I'm not in church for a couple of weeks. It's not that big a deal if I give in to this one temptation. I really don't have what it takes to serve God in that way. I'm too weary to hold on any longer.* We need constant encouragement in the truth. Scripture gives us exhortations to encourage our brothers and sisters, examples of holy encouragement, and lists of the fruit that encouragement produces.

The writer to the Hebrews tells us that encouragement is a more powerful way to promote holiness than we may think. It really makes a difference.

> Watch out, brothers and sisters, so that there won't be in any of you an evil, unbelieving heart that turns away from the living God. But encourage each other daily, while it is still called today, so that none of you is hardened by sin's deception. For we have become participants in Christ if we hold firmly until the end the reality that we had at the start. (Heb. 3:12–14 csb)

We are to encourage each other in the Word. Let us encourage one another in holiness.

As advocates, we encourage our siblings before others as well. Barnabas, whose name means "son of encouragement," was known for this. He encouraged the apostles by selling a field so that all the money could be used for his brothers and sisters in God's household (see Acts 4:36–37). When the disciples were fearful of Paul, Barnabas advocated for him, persuading them that Paul's ministry was from God. He encouraged Paul's apostleship. He also spoke up for a fellow disciple who had momentarily waivered but was ready to serve again. He pleaded with Paul to take John Mark with them on their travels to strengthen the churches, but Paul wasn't convinced that John Mark wouldn't desert them again. Barnabas was so adamant to encourage his brother John Mark in God's work that he and Paul split ways.

We see the fruit of Barnabas' investment in promoting John Mark's holiness and the work he did for the church. John Mark and Paul restored their relationship, and Paul called John Mark a fellow worker and requested his presence because of how useful he was in the ministry (see Col. 4:10; 2 Tim. 4:11;

Philem. 24). And John Mark wrote one of the four gospels in the canon of Scripture.

Everyone needs encouragement—even leaders. This should be our daily practice with one another. But encouragement should only be exercised in the truth. Our culture values positive speak that doesn't necessarily have to be congruent with reality. That isn't real encouragement. Our esteem is based on who made us and what we are made for. It isn't self-centered but Christ-centered. We don't downplay our weaknesses; we acknowledge them and look to Christ for our strength. That is our encouragement. And we don't pursue every dream we can think up, but we ask for wisdom and discernment to walk in God's will for us, knowing our common mission for the household of God. Sacred siblings encourage in true hope, not through shallow platitudes.

Practicing Exhortation

Encouragement and exhortation are two sides of the same coin. Both of them share the goal of promoting holiness. Encouragement gives support and stimulates courage so the recipient can act on true hope. Exhortation involves stronger imploring and is often accompanied by warnings if the exhortation isn't heeded. Exhortation can be toward a positive action or against a negative action or sin. It draws a line in the sand. While exhortation often includes encouragement, it beseeches a more immediate response. Scripture is full of exhortations.

Sometimes we need to hear plain rebuke or stronger urging to obedience. But we need exhortation not merely when we are tempted or falling into sin. As with encouragement, we need exhortation all the time. While affirming their faithful living, Paul exhorts the Thessalonian brothers and sisters to continue "even more" in obedience to the faith (see 1 Thess. 4:1–2). As he calls them to continue in sanctification, Paul gets more specific. His exhortations teach us once again what we are called to and how we are to treat our siblings.

> For this is God's will, your sanctification: that you keep away from sexual immorality, that each of you knows how to control his own body in holiness and honor, not with lustful passions, like the Gentiles, who don't know God. This means one must not transgress against and take advantage of a brother or sister in this manner, because the Lord is an avenger of all these offenses, as we also previously told and warned you. For God has not called us to impurity but to live in holiness. Consequently, anyone who rejects this does not reject man, but God, who gives you his Holy Spirit. (1 Thess. 4:3–8 csb)

Paul continues to affirm that the Thessalonian brothers and sisters love one another well, but then he exhorts them to show this love "even more," giving practical ways they can do that (see vv. 9–12). Instead of saying that men and women can't be friends, he exhorts men and women to holiness and a sacred siblingship that will help them to honor one another and exercise self-control.

Sermons are also exhortations, and they carry the authority of God (see Heb. 13:22). So not only do we need to hear both encouragement and exhortation from our brothers and sisters, we need to regularly assemble together to sit under the preaching of the Word.

Practicing Intercession

We've seen that our Elder Brother intercedes to the heavenly Father on our behalf. Like him, we need to intercede for one another. We are to do this both corporately, as the household of God, and personally for our brothers and sisters. Dietrich Bonhoeffer calls intercession for one another the "pulsing heart of all Christian life in unison," defining it as prayer for our siblings that brings them "into the presence of God" and sees them "under the Cross of Jesus as . . . poor human being[s] and sinner[s] in need of grace."[13] This isn't an option for God's people. "A Christian fellowship lives and exists by the intercession of its members for one another, or it collapses."[14]

Bonhoeffer explains how intercessory prayer for our brothers and sisters changes the way that we view them, overcoming the hatred, tension, or intolerance we may have previously had toward them. Once we bring them into the presence of God, we look at them as God sees them in Jesus Christ. When we pray for our brothers and sisters, we follow in the steps of our Elder Brother and become more like him. This can be a struggle for us to do sometimes, as Bonhoeffer doesn't deny, but it is a transforming one.

Knowing this Christian responsibility and practicing it regularly positions us as trusted brothers and sisters when a sibling needs a safe person to confess her sins to or to ask for personal prayer. James affirms this: "Confess your sins to one another and pray for one another, so that you may be healed. The prayer of a righteous person is very powerful in its effect" (James 5:16 csb). Isn't that an encouraging exhortation? We are encouraged in holiness so that we can have confidence that our prayers are powerful; we can turn to our righteous brothers and sisters and ask for prayer, knowing that their prayers are powerful too. Intercession isn't a practice that we are to

---

13. Dietrich Bonhoeffer, *Life Together* (New York: Harper & Row, 1954), 86.
14. Bonhoeffer, 86.

keep to ourselves; we are called to seek the prayers of our brothers and sisters and to pray for them as well.

Stronger and Weaker Siblings

On some issues our faith may be stronger or weaker than our brothers' or sisters', and we are responsible to take care "never to put a stumbling block or pitfall in the way of [our] brother or sister" (Rom. 14:13 CSB). We exercise our faith in different areas, and some of us have more liberty that comes with a stronger knowledge of or conscientiousness in the faith.

Paul addresses this issue in Romans 14 and 1 Corinthians 8. He probably needs to mention it more than once because this is an area in which siblings often have less patience and care for one another. Paul brings up some issues that were troubling Christians then. Could they eat meat? Could they eat meat sacrificed to idols? Was it okay to celebrate Jewish holy days? Then he exhorts them to

> accept anyone who is weak in faith, but don't argue about disputed matters. One person believes he may eat anything, while one who is weak eats only vegetables. One who eats must not look down on one who does not eat, and one who does not eat must not judge one who does, because God has accepted him. Who are you to judge another's household servant? Before his own Lord he stands or falls. And he will stand, because the Lord is able to make him stand. (Rom. 14:1–4 CSB)

See how Paul uses household language here. We are to look at our brothers and sisters as they stand in God's household. In one sense Paul offers resolution to these differences of conviction, in that he says that the stronger sibling understands there is liberty in these matters. But he tells stronger siblings not to look down on those whose consciences are weaker. Don't try to force a brother or sister's conscience, because you will be a stumbling block to them. If they think it is sinful to eat meat, then you are unloving to require them to do so. Those with the weaker faith in these matters do feel strong convictions about them.

These are not make-or-break kingdom of God issues, so Paul requires us to show love and forbearance. That is not always easy for a sibling to do. Paul points out that in these matters, everyone is doing what they think will best glorify God. "Whoever observes the day, observes it for the honor of the Lord. Whoever eats, eats for the Lord. . . . But you, why do you judge your brother or sister?" (Rom. 14:6, 10 CSB).

If our liberties cause our brothers or sisters to stumble, we who are stronger in the faith should sacrifice our rights out of love and care for our siblings. Paul gives strong words to the Corinthians: "Now when you sin like this against brothers and sisters and wound their weak conscience, you are sinning against Christ" (1 Cor. 8:12 CSB). Strength comes with sibling responsibility. Food, drink, and Jewish holy days might not be a serious matter, but our responsibility to one another *is* a serious matter in God's household.

Practicing Men and Women

Notice that the practices mentioned in this chapter are for both brothers and sisters to exercise together. Encouragement isn't a feminine practice that is reserved for women's ministries, and intercession isn't a masculine practice that squeezes out the women. These are household practices that men and women exercise corporately and in their personal friendships with one another. These practices put godly friendship in its proper tracks toward holiness. Those are very different tracks from what much of the evangelical culture has laid down for how men and women should relate.

Promoting holiness in a sibling presupposes discernment of his or her strengths and weaknesses. Natural siblings are really good at this, aren't they? Selfish siblings will capitalize on another sibling's weakness and compete with his strengths. Immature siblings point out flaws, compete to have one up over each other, and taunt, rather than encourage and exhort. This isn't good behavior, of course—but, even when there is negative behavior, siblings in a healthy household know that the relationship is fundamentally loving.

When it comes to relationships between the sexes, we don't combat evil with constant suspicion, regulations, and avoidance. In fact, we sin when we allow a ruling passion or sensual desire to determine our relationships, grieving the Holy Spirit and quenching his work to develop the affection of godly siblingship.[15] While it's necessary to establish proper boundaries with those who relate in a sinful manner, we must also know the proper way to relate with our brothers and sisters. Knowing what is good builds our discernment. Promoting what is good invests in the holiness of others. "Brothers and sisters, . . . be infants in regard to evil and adult in your thinking" (1 Cor. 14:20 csb).

We are called to love. That means that we want to sharpen the strengths of our siblings, that we do not put stumbling blocks in their areas of weakness, and that we participate in their growth in holiness. That is what our Elder Brother does for us and what we are called to do for one another. Instilling and modeling practices that promote holiness directs us to the maturity that we are called to. It gives us concrete ways to

15. Thanks again to Dave Myers for this line.

relate to one another at a time when we are seeing Hollywood producers, famous actors, politicians, and even Christian leaders exposed for sexual harassment and rape.

Discussion Questions

1. How does your own busy schedule or personal ambition hinder your gratitude? Do you recognize gifts as interruptions? Do you sometimes see Sunday as an interruption to your "real life"? Are you hesitant to publicly recognize any of your friends? Do you think that is because you are ungrateful for this gift of friendship or because theirs is not a holy friendship?
2. How does encouragement differ from flattery? How does exhortation differ from condemnation?
3. What practice outlined in this chapter do you think you need to exercise more in order to promote holy sibling friendships? What can you do as a practical first step?

11

Enjoy Table Fellowship Together

Long before the Billy Graham Rule, we were making an issue out of who we eat with. Your lunch partner was an even bigger deal in the Jerusalem society during Jesus' time—so much so that Robert Karris and others have argued that "Jesus got himself crucified by the way he ate."[1]

In Jerusalem, your dinner companions impacted not only your social status but your actual righteousness. Jewish society kept a very rigorous, "detailed description of those considered to be ethnically pure Israelites . . . to determine who was worthy to engage in table fellowship with them. Anyone not worthy . . . was considered a sinner, and the categories of sinner were long and detailed."[2] So when an immoral woman crashed the meal at a Pharisee's house, wetted Jesus' feet with her own tears, and wiped them with her hair, it wasn't surprising that

1. Robert J. Karris, *Luke: Artist and Theologian; Luke's Passion Account as Literature* (Eugene, OR: Wipf & Stock, 1985), 47.
2. Arthur A. Just Jr., *The Ongoing Feast: Table Fellowship and Eschatology at Emmaus* (Collegeville, MN: The Liturgical Press, 1993), 132.

the host was pretty disturbed (see Luke 7:36–50). I wonder how close this woman was to being the absolute worst person to be seen with at a meal. Then imagine the uproar when Jesus was spotted supping with Levi the tax collector. We are talking about the dregs of society.

Even children and teenagers care about their dining companions. If you don't sit at the "cool table," you at least try not to sit at that *other* table—the loser table full of misfits. Yet that's the table where Jesus usually took his seat. He began attracting "all the tax collectors and the sinners" so that they "were coming near Him to listen to Him" (Luke 15:1). And more Pharisees and scribes murmured, saying, "This man receives sinners and eats with them" (v. 2).

Food and table fellowship are major themes in the gospel of Luke. If Jesus isn't eating and drinking with sinners, it seems like he's talking about eating and drinking in his parables. "Jesus is either going to a meal, at a meal, or coming from a meal. . . . The aroma of food issues forth from each and every chapter of Luke's Gospel."[3] Luke knows that there is meaning attached to whom we eat with, and Jesus made many unlikely friends and enemies this way.

In the present age, Christ's table is inclusive. His invitation goes out to all sinners and misfits, including us. What does this imply concerning our attitude toward those we eat with? In Jesus' day, "those who shared in the same food and drink were regarded as sharing in the same blood and the same principle of life, and thus bound to each other by a sacred bond."[4] That sounds a lot like siblingship, doesn't it? "Table-fellowship was a

3. Karris, *Luke*, 47.
4. Louis F. Hartman, trans., *Encyclopedic Dictionary of the Bible: A Translation and Adaptation of Adrianus van den Born's* Woordenboek, 2nd rev. ed. (New York: McGraw-Hill, 1963), 2080–81.

guarantee of peace, trust, brotherhood; it meant in a very real sense a sharing of one's life."[5]

If your high school days are behind you, you're probably thankful that you no longer have to think about which table to sit at when you eat. But are you mindful of sharing fellowship at the table with your brothers and sisters in Christ? Do you consider how dining with an unbeliever, someone who is still in his or her sins, can be a good, evangelical exercise? Hospitality builds stronger community; so, in this chapter, I'll focus on welcoming others using table fellowship.

Eyes Wide Open

In one of the most fascinating accounts in Scripture. Luke tells us about the two disciples walking from Jerusalem to Emmaus who were distressed by Christ's crucifixion and the news that he had risen from the dead. Jesus approached them, but "their eyes were prevented from recognizing Him" (Luke 24:16).

When he asked why they were so upset, the disciples couldn't believe that anyone in Jerusalem would be so uninformed. But, when they explained the situation, Jesus rebuked them for not knowing the Scriptures. Even after being part of Jesus' ministry, the two disciples were oblivious. They thought they were sharing the latest news, but they didn't know what they were talking about. So, as they walked the seven miles together, Jesus Christ himself gave his disciples the sermon of a lifetime about how all the Scriptures point to him. All the while, they didn't realize that they were talking with the Messiah.

Once they reached their destination, the disciples insisted

5. James D. G. Dunn, *Unity and Diversity in the New Testament: An Inquiry into the Character of Earliest Christianity* (London: SCM Press, 1977), 162; see also Hartman, 2080–81.

that Jesus stay with them, inviting him to the table to eat. Then things got even crazier. Jesus took over as the host, taking the bread, blessing it, and giving it to the disciples.

> Then their eyes were opened and they recognized Him; and He vanished from their sight. They said to one another, "Were not our hearts burning within us while He was speaking to us on the road, while He was explaining the Scriptures to us?" (Luke 24:31–32)

In this amazing account, Jesus preaches the Word, fellowships at the table, and then blesses and breaks the bread. In his book *The Ongoing Feast*, Arthur Just Jr. argues that this is the first fulfillment of Jesus' command during the Last Supper, "Do this in remembrance of me."[6] Immediately after the resurrection, we see Jesus again with bread and wine, leading his disciples to worshipful remembrance.

In Scripture we see table fellowship as a means to celebrate, to remember, and to look forward. Just notes that feasts in Scripture are liturgical events at which God's people recognize his presence with them while rehearsing remembrance of the work he has done for their salvation.[7] The meal at Emmaus culminates *all* God's covenant fellowship with his people in *all* the meals they have celebrated with him— particularly the Passover meal and the Last Supper. The Emmaus meal also signals the continuation of the practice of table fellowship between redeemed sinners and their Savior.[8]

But there's more. The language describing the Emmaus meal contrasts with another eye-opening eating encounter in Scripture. Just focuses on Luke's literary presentation of this

---

6. See Just, *The Ongoing Feast*, 241–42.
7. See Just, 241.
8. See Just, 241–42.

Emmaus account in "concentric circles," or rings. The center of the circle represents the climax, and the verses that lead up to and follow it are like rings with parallel points. Here is a helpful illustration of this chiasm given by the author:

> 5) v. 13 "That very day two of them were going . . . from Jerusalem"
>> 4) v. 14 ". . . and talking with each other . . ."
>>> 3) v. 15 ". . . Jesus himself drew near and went with them."
>>>> 2) v. 16 "But their eyes were kept from recognizing him."
>>>>> 1) vv. 17–30 (the center circle) "the colloquium and breaking of the bread"
>>>> 2) v. 31a "And their eyes were opened and they recognized him."
>>> 3) v. 31b ". . . and he vanished out of their sight."
>> 4) v. 32 "They said to each other . . ."
> 5) v. 33 "And they arose that same hour and returned to Jerusalem."[9]

Notice the second ring, in which the disciples' eyes were first closed (i.e., kept from recognizing Jesus) and then opened. Does that sound familiar? The same language is used to describe Adam and Eve in Genesis 3:7: "The eyes of both of them were opened."

The open eyes of Adam and Eve are the first expression of the fallen creation that now sees the image of God clouded by disobedience; the open eyes of the Emmaus disciples are

---

9. Just, 31. The original chiasm contained Greek text as well, which I have removed for clarity.

the first expression of the new creation that now sees the image restored in the new Adam, the crucified and risen Christ. This is a clear link between the old and new creations, establishing the Emmaus meal as an eschatological event.[10]

When we share in the covenant meal of the Lord's Supper, we are given a special means of grace that conveys Christ and all his blessings to us. The one meal reverses the other so that our eyes too are opened to "see in Jesus the seed of the woman promised in Genesis 3:15. The table at which [the disciples] now sit is the messianic table. Just as Adam and Eve's eating of the forbidden fruit was the first meal of the fallen creation, so this meal at Emmaus is the first meal of the new creation on the first day of the week."[11]

In the fascinating account of the disciples in Emmaus, we have the vision of the fulfillment of God's promise to Adam and Eve. The Christ is made known in his exposition of Scripture on their walk and in the breaking of bread. Boom: eyes wide open! What we may think of as common, ordinary means are used to confer Christ and all his blessings.

Dress Rehearsals at the Table

While we shouldn't limit our table fellowship to an exclusive group, there will be some regulars who we enjoy having around. It's okay to have favorite dining partners. Even Jesus did.

I particularly love to feast with my extended family. I've always been very close with my parents and siblings, and it is such a blessing that we all love the Lord. We particularly

10. Just, 66–67.
11. Just, 67.

look forward to combining all our families as we share one of the more meaningful feasts of the year together: Thanksgiving. But we also have some different convictions about things, and this becomes very apparent around the table. Matt and I are Presbyterians, my brother-in-law and sister are associated with the Anglican Church in North America (ACNA), and my brother and his wife go to a non-denominational church. So you can imagine that we have some differing views about worship and some of the doctrines of the church. Since we are all passionate about our faith, these differences are certainly noticed. And we don't tend to be small talkers, so we enjoy passionate conversations around the table. Thankfully, we are in harmony about the primary confessions of the faith, and we try not to be too irritating when we disagree about the secondary stuff.

Along with this, we also have different ideas about food. All of us are avid about health, yet this itself manifests in different ways. This became apparent during one particular Thanksgiving meal. There we were, one loving, thankful family, representing a gamut of nutritional and dining convictions. We had your strictly plant-based eaters, the organic and non-GMO campaigners, some with nut allergies, those with the conviction to back off gluten, and your atypical mom who has free-range chickens just because it's kind of awesome. Mom arrived with the fresh turkey ordered from the same local dairy farm where she gets her cream, butter, and coffee beans.

Sometimes I get uncomfortable when I anticipate our eating together. Can we come together, with our strong convictions, and still truly enjoy one another's company? How can we feast together on Thanksgiving when we don't even eat the same food? Since we are all so vehement about the convictions that we hold, they aren't easily put aside. There may even be some food proselytizing going on, as well as some articulate defenses of our views. But these are joyous times, because I have one of the most awesome families around. I enjoy being with some of the people I love the most, who know more about me than many do and who love me anyway. We have a wonderful ability to move from serious, intelligent conversation, to silly outbursts of fun, to nunchuck lessons. And that's just the adults.

We eat ordinary meals with others on a regular basis. We partake in the Lord's Supper, a means of grace through which ordinary bread and wine convey the benefits of Jesus' death and resurrection to his people. But we also look forward to feasting with our Savior on that Great Day when our Lord returns. God's Word invites us to the marriage supper of the Lamb—the great feast that the bride of Christ will have with her Groom on the day of consummation. People will "come from east and west and from north and south, and will recline at the table in the kingdom of God" (Luke 13:29). Isn't it significant that the first event we are promised on the new earth is a feast with Jesus and our siblings?

My family's Thanksgiving meals are *proleptic meals*— microcosmic pictures of what is to come. Christ's people will serve and worship our great Lord for eternity, but our first business is a feast of thanksgiving and celebration. We will be overwhelmed with gratitude for our great reward, Christ himself. Despite the diverse people gathered together, there will be no tension, no anxiety over which foods to eat together. Christ will serve the feast himself.

At my Thanksgiving table, a bunch of redeemed sinners who love the Lord gather to share the blessings that our God has lavished on us. In this act, we both proclaim God's redeeming love and look forward to reclining at Christ's table with many from the east, west, north, and south. All our table fellowship is proleptic in this way. The future feast with Christ is so real that we share its blessings when we gather together in the present. Our smaller meals are microcosms of the great one to come.

How does this affect your views of hospitality and Christian fellowship? Have you ever considered that the meals you have with those in your church are proleptic? The early Christians got themselves into some trouble during their love feasts (see 1 Cor. 11:17–26)—partly because they didn't think about how that feast points to the great feast that we will all enjoy together. Do we make that connection now? Do we even bother to eat together? Do we consider the presence of Christ at the table?

Our Daily Bread

People who worry about eating with the other sex are on to something. When we sit at a table to eat together, the dynamic is very different from eating alone. But we need to be careful not to mistake the intimacy of fellowship with romantic sexuality. When we sit with our brothers and sisters in Christ for a meal, we rehearse for our eternal life in the new heavens and the new earth. Having lunch shouldn't feel like a challenge to marital fidelity. Eating together is a platonic practice intended to bring joy to our friendships. Table talk is not the same as pillow talk, so let's not treat it that way.

Christian brothers and sisters share a practice at the beginning of their meals that sets the scene perfectly. We give thanks to God for our food, and we ask for his blessing on it. Like the two disciples on the road to Emmaus, we ask Jesus to join us for a meal. And that changes everything.

Theologian Dietrich Bonhoeffer shared three things about the act of giving thanks that build Christian community.[12]

12. See Dietrich Bonhoeffer, *Life Together* (New York: Harper & Row, 1954), 66–69.

- When we give thanks for our daily food, we acknowledge that we are receivers and renounce our own self-reliance. With grateful hearts we recognize God as the giver and thank him for our food.
- The fellowship that we share around the table is Christocentric. God's gifts are given to us through Christ and for his sake. The gifts that we enjoy remind us of the greatest gift, which God has not withheld from us. So in giving thanks and fellowshipping over a meal, we join with the Father, through the Spirit, in the love of our greater blessing, Jesus Christ. This gladdens our hearts!
- We invoke God's presence with us at the meal in full confidence that he accepts us. As we look to the "true Bread of life itself," we celebrate rest from and sustenance after our labors, remembering "the One who is calling [us] to the banquet of the Kingdom of God. So in a singular way, that daily table fellowship binds the Christians to their Lord and one another. At table they know their Lord as the one who breaks bread for them; the eyes of their faith are opened."[13]

Sharing the blessing of ordinary meals deepens our communion in the Lord—just through our daily practice of eating around a table! Since we set the table dynamic with a prayer over our meal and our time together, our conversations should flourish as though Christ were sitting with us—not as a chaperone, but as our friend who is not afraid to eat with sinners.

"The table fellowship of Christians implies obligation. It is *our* daily bread that we eat, not my own. We share our bread."[14] This means that we care about not only the spiritual

13. Bonhoeffer, 67–68.
14. Bonhoeffer, 68.

needs of others but their physical needs as well. Table fellowship is a practice that cares for others.

How well are we modeling this at the table? Are we sharing our gifts and time by inviting brothers and sisters to our table? Are we paying attention to whether any of our siblings are in need, from hunger or loneliness? Are we mindful of our prayers? Is the substance of our prayers reflected in our conversation and conduct? Are we after our own glory when we are hospitable?

Sharing Tables

Table fellowship extends grace and strengthens community. It is a loving way to take care of our family, so we should continually practice it with our siblings in Christ. But table fellowship is also a way of connecting with the lost. In his book *A Meal with Jesus*, Tim Chester argues that table fellowship is a great practice for sharing the life of Christ with others. "We all have to eat. Three meals a day, seven days a week. That's twenty-one opportunities for mission and community without adding anything to your schedule."[15] Sometimes it's necessary to eat alone. But our "to go" culture has normalized eating in our cars or in front of the computer rather than pausing from our day to dine, share, and reflect at the table—even at work.

In fact, the workplace often provides regular opportunities to get to know someone more by sharing a table and some food for twenty minutes or so. We could build relationships with fellow believers in the workforce, or we could get to know more people who do not know Christ. What if we are the only expression of Christianity in their lives?

---

15. Tim Chester, *A Meal with Jesus: Discovering Grace, Community, and Mission around the Table* (Wheaton, IL: Crossway: 2011), 92.

Christ's interaction with sinners, especially around the table, creates a new kind of community. This community doesn't invite someone to the table for selfish reasons but in order to live out gospel truths. "Sharing tables is one of the most uniquely human things we do. No other creature consumes its food at a table. And sharing tables with other people reminds us that there's more to food than fuel. We don't eat only for sustenance."[16] When we join someone for a meal, we do theology too.[17] We take time to receive, bless, share, rehearse truths, and create history together.

In our new community, we don't look for the seat of honor at the table, and we do look to invite people who can't repay us the favor (see Luke 14:7–14). The table is not a place to clamor for advancement; it is a place for humility. We are all receivers at Christ's table. We can never repay him for his generosity to us. So, as we pray for him to bless our food and fellowship, we bless others in turn, hoping to see more redeemed sinners ushered into Christ's great banquet.

Sharing a table can raise eyebrows sometimes. In Jesus' day, food was a boundary marker that kept outsiders away. But since Christ has fulfilled all the purity laws of Leviticus, "grace can't be integrated with self-righteousness and self-importance. It's radically different, radically new."[18] Yet we still struggle with this over two thousand years later. We use the table to distance ourselves from those who may harm our reputation, whether they are members of the other sex or unbelievers who aren't as polished as we are. Heck, we can

---

16. Barry D. Jones, "A Place at the Table," *DTS Magazine* 1, no. 1 (Fall 2015): 11. Available online at http://issuu.com/dallasseminary/docs/dts-magazine-fall -2015?e=4615024/30420252.

17. See Chester, *A Meal with Jesus*, 21.

18. Chester, 26.

even distance ourselves while sitting right next to someone and eating completely different things.[19]

The Billy Graham rule arose out of a common fear in evangelism that meeting one-on-one at the table with the other sex comes with a stigma—the Billy Crystal stigma. Does the sex part always get in the way? Could the intimacy of sharing a meal lead to sexual sin? Well, to rephrase the title of an article on a similar topic, affairs don't start with lunch.[20] Table fellowship doesn't cause affairs. Sexual impropriety arises from affections that are not rightly ordered. When this is the case, then yes, ordinary activities such as lunch, texting, and traveling in the same car can be avenues for bad behavior. But the table isn't the problem. The problem is the heart.

Mature people seek table fellowship regularly. They don't plot to be alone with the other sex just for the sake of it, but they also shouldn't be suspect if they share a meal with a man or a woman. The blessing that Christians pray together before sharing a meal sets the dynamic at the table and invites their Lord to be with them.

Eating together is provocative in Scripture, but not for romantic reasons. Over and over again, we see the disciples exhorted to share food and to join in table fellowship. We see Jesus and his followers looking for opportunities for table fellowship. We see mealtimes being used to learn about people and to teach the gospel. As Jesus and his disciples eat, they break down old boundary markers so that the table becomes as generously inclusive as the gospel call itself.

---

19. See David Lertis Matson, "Personalized vs. Parallel Eating: Luke's Challenge for the 21st Century Church," *Leaven* 20, no. 1 (spring 2012), available online at https://digitalcommons.pepperdine.edu/cgi/viewcontent.cgi?article=2160& context=leaven.

20. See Sarah Taras and Jon Wymer, "Affairs Don't Start with Texts," *Just One Train Wreck after Another* (blog), March 20, 2017, https://timfall.wordpress.com /2017/03/20/affairs-dont-start-for-with-texts/.

When Not to Share Tables

It's interesting to note that the Bible never warns us that sharing a meal with the other sex will lead to an affair. We aren't told that we may catch atheism or sin by joining an unbeliever at the table. But we *are* told not to fellowship with a false brother or sister—one who claims to be united to Christ while living an immoral lifestyle (see 1 Cor. 5:9–13). While exhorting us not to associate with a false sibling, Paul adds, "Do not *even eat* with such a person" (v. 11).

This additional restriction points to table fellowship as being a Christian social custom, not a taboo practice. It's actually a form of discipline to remove a confessing believer who is living in sin from table fellowship. The biblical parameters of when to be exclusive at our tables should be our parameters as well.

Remember that in the final judgment, many who think they will eat with Jesus will not be invited to the wedding feast. "He will say, 'I tell you, I do not know where you are from; depart from Me, all you evildoers.' In that place there will be weeping and gnashing of teeth when you see Abraham and Isaac and Jacob and all the prophets in the kingdom of God, but yourselves being thrown out" (Luke 13:27–28). These are startling words. If we value table fellowship rightly, we will not entertain a lie around the table. Therefore, we are not to tolerate false siblings at the table.

It is interesting that the table is the very place where Jesus calls out a false sibling. At the Last Supper we have another scene involving bread and revelation (see John 13:21–30). Jesus announces to his disciples that someone at the table will be his betrayer. As they are all anxious to know who it is, Jesus says that it is the one to whom he will give a dipped morsel of bread. As he gives the bread to Judas, he tells him to act quickly. Judas immediately leaves the table and the feast.

When We Get Up from the Table

When it comes to sharing a table together, there's a lot for us to think about regarding our everyday lives and our practices in worship. The Bible encourages us to exercise the powerful relational practice of eating together. Our shared meals are powerful because of their proleptic nature. With the breaking of bread, there is a breaking in of Christ's everlasting kingdom—right at the table. The future breaks in to the present; the age to come breaks in to these last days.

When we eat together, we enact gospel truths and participate in daily moments in which we are bound to our Lord and to one another.[21] The King is summoning a people to his table. The world may think that a rejected Savior has invited us to a table full of outcasts. It certainly looks odd that we feast on our Savior's body and blood. But because of his body and blood, there will come a day when we are invited to the great feast, in which "Christ will be the *host* rather than the *meal* and we will eat and drink *with* him in an everlasting exchange of gifts."[22] "Blessed are those who are invited to the marriage supper of the Lamb" (Rev. 19:9).

Time in table fellowship is a special time. While we don't transport ourselves to another dimension like the characters in *A Wrinkle in Time*, Charles Wallace is on to something when he says that "a straight line is not the shortest distance between two points."[23] Our tables are a wrinkle in time that connects us to heaven and opens our eyes to the joyful reality of the age to come. And when we spend our time well in table fellowship,

21. See Bonhoeffer, *Life Together*, 67.

22. Michael Horton, *The Gospel-Driven Life: Being Good News People in a Bad News World* (Grand Rapids: Baker Books, 2009), 242.

23. Madeleine L'Engle, *A Wrinkle in Time* (New York: Farrar, Straus and Giroux, 1962; repr., New York: Square Fish, 2007), 88.

we get up from the table with an anticipation and affirmation that even unbelievers can't shake: "Blessed is everyone who will eat bread in the kingdom of God!" (Luke 14:15).

Discussion Questions

1. Have you thought much before about a theology of table fellowship? How is table fellowship a practice that promotes holiness?
2. How does giving thanks and asking for blessing in prayer before a meal "set the table" for good table fellowship?
3. How can you practice table fellowship as a way to connect with the lost (unbelievers)? In what practical ways can you implement this into your family or work schedule? How is this different from sharing table fellowship with a false sibling?

12

Celebrate and Suffer Together

If I had to use only one word to describe sibling relationships, I would choose *solidarity*. Jesus appeals to family solidarity when he says, "If anyone comes to Me, and does not hate his own father and mother and wife and children and brothers and sisters, yes, and even his own life, he cannot be My disciple" (Luke 14:26). He isn't telling us that we should hate our families; he is emphasizing that our union with Christ is so strong that our solidarity is in him now, even over our biological families. Solidarity offers physical protection and care, but it is also expressed in emotional support and companionship. Siblings are supposed to be the people in your life whom you are able to count on.

We've seen that antiquity placed a lot of value in the bond between siblings. Nowadays we place more emphasis on marital solidarity. Contemporary stories, books, movies, and music often represent our cultural consensus that the worst form of betrayal is spousal. But Greek mythology, Scripture, and other ancient literature depict the ultimate betrayal as one enacted by a sibling:

The story of Cain's murder of his brother Abel was told frequently by Second Temple Israelites and early Christians to illustrate the extreme possibilities of human wickedness. . . . The Roman poet Ovid (early first-century C.E.) supported his judgment about the extreme breakdown of social relations during the late Roman Republic by pointing out that "friend was not safe from friend . . . and even between brothers affection was rare" ([Metamorphoses]1.127–51). Thus readers of Mark's gospel could grasp immediately the seriousness of the warning that as God's judgment approached, social relations would become so badly broken that "brother will hand brother over to death" (Mark 13:12).[1]

Even now, the term *sibling rivalry* has strong emotional connotations. Is there a worse rivalry than sibling rivalry?

Although it isn't inspired Scripture, the apocryphal book of Jubilees sums this up well. When Rebecca, believing that she is near death, pleads with her son Esau to promise her that he will not kill his brother after her passing, Esau gives a convicting reply:

Jacob, my brother, also, I shall love above all flesh; for I have not a brother in all the earth but him only: and this is no great merit for me if I love him; for he is my brother, and we were sown together in thy body, and together came we forth from thy womb, and if I do not love my brother, whom shall I love? (Jubilees 35:22)

1. S. Scott Bartchy, "The Sibling Secret (Revealed)," *Leaven* 9, no. 1 (Winter 2001): 19–20, https://digitalcommons.pepperdine.edu/cgi/viewcontent.cgi?article=1531&context=leaven. He gives 4 Maccabees 18:11; Testament of Benjamin 7:5; 1 John 3:12; Jude 11; 1 Clement 4:17; Josephus Antiquities 1.52–66 as supporting references.

This poetic description of solidarity ironically comes from a player in one of the most infamous sibling rivalries. Esau says that he loves Jacob for who he is: his brother. If he can't love his own brother, who in the world *can* he love?

In this chapter, we will look at how the practices of celebrating and suffering together form a shared history and solidarity, both then and now. These are practices that standout siblings do well. Rivals cannot bear to share in celebrating another sibling's success. And, rather than bearing one another's burdens, rivals find pleasure in one another's suffering or react to it with indifference.

Celebrating Life and Restoration

As Job is argued to be one of the oldest books in Scripture, one of the earliest things recorded in the inspired Word of God is a celebration between brothers and sisters. The second sentence in Job introduces us to these seven brothers and three sisters, and the fourth sentence tells us about the feasts that each of the brothers hosted "on his day" (Job 1:4)—likely their birthdays. So, in the opening description of Job's blessedness, we see that his children celebrated their lives together. At the end of the book, following his many trials, Job celebrates his restoration with his own brothers and sisters.

In Jesus' parable of the prodigal son (Luke 15:11–32), the prodigal son is not blameless like Job.[2] The younger of two brothers, he asks for his inheritance before his father's death and squanders it with "loose living" (v. 13). Once his funds run dry, he returns home remorseful and repentant, and the father responds with great celebration—ostentatious celebration that

2. Job isn't a parable, but we can make observations about celebrations between siblings in both accounts.

provokes bitterness and self-righteousness in the older brother. The older brother's anger hinders him from joining in. He cannot celebrate his own brother's restoration.

The father comes out to plead with him, giving an explanation that leaves no room for the brother to opt out: "But we *had* to celebrate and rejoice, for this brother of yours was dead and has begun to live, and was lost and has been found" (v. 32). This is way better than a birthday celebration. The father is talking about spiritual life! Siblings *have* to celebrate life! They've been doing it as far back as Scripture has been written!

We still celebrate both life and restoration today, and when it comes to birthdays, weddings, or new babies, siblings are usually on the guest list. How much more should we celebrate new life in Christ! As exciting as it is to bring a new baby into the world, how much more marvelous is it to celebrate spiritual life in the kingdom of God?

The parable of the prodigal son convicts me as a sibling in Christ. The main thrust of the parable leads me to examine my self-righteous heart. That nails me for sure. But it also makes me think about how little a deal we often make over a restored sinner or a new life in Christ. These are amazing works of God that call for great rejoicing and celebration. While we do rejoice when we see someone come to Christ and join our family, how meager are our celebrations? The father in the parable didn't hold back. That's what makes the older brother so jealous. He whips out the fatted calf and clothes the restored brother with a swanky robe, bling, and a new pair of sandals, and the music and dancing can be heard from outside the house. That's a heck of a celebration! Maybe the church could improve in this area for both our new and restored siblings.

Notice all the feasting going on in these celebrations. Table fellowship is always a part of them. What would a baby shower be like with no food? And accompanying expressions of celebration serve to personalize the occasion. At a baby shower I recently attended, we celebrated both the mom and the baby in two special ways. The mother, Joli, is the eldest of seven sisters, and their sibling love and solidarity was beautiful to see. One of the sisters played a song that she wrote, celebrating all the ways that Joli has touched all her sisters' lives. It was a beautiful expression of Joli as a life-giver. Then her mother asked her how we could pray for Joli and her baby, and we all joined in prayer to do just that. These personal touches to the celebration of new life expressed the fruit of our solidarity with Joli and also built on that solidarity to make it stronger.

This is something to think about in our own celebrations. Do we just go through the motions in obligatory fashion, or do we truly express our gratitude and joy for the occasion? This recent baby shower really made me think about how godly celebration publicly acknowledges that our gifts, opportunities, physical and spiritual lives, restoration, and accomplishments are all from the Lord, through the Lord, and offered back to the Lord in thanksgiving. Siblings in Christ should be known as a celebrating people.

Solidarity in Suffering

Christians also practice suffering. That sounds strange. Do we really need to *practice* suffering? We welcome reasons to celebrate, and we practice celebration with parties, feasts, singing, and prayer, and in many other creative ways. But we do not welcome reasons to suffer. We do not want our siblings to suffer. We pray for relief from and removal of suffering, knowing that our sovereign God can deliver us now and absolutely will deliver us completely upon his return. In the new heavens and the new earth, there will be no suffering; but as long as sin remains, so will the curse. So while siblings in Christ don't invoke suffering for ourselves or one another, we all still experience it.[3] And, when we do, how do we practice suffering as Christian siblings? How do we *do* suffering? More particularly, how do we build sibling solidarity in suffering? Loving siblings often fall short here.

First, we need to listen. Again, the book of Job offers a strong illustration of this. After the loss of his children, his wealth, and his health, Job's wife tells him to toss his integrity out the window and to "curse God and die!" (Job 2:9). Job is totally alone in his suffering, sitting in the city landfill. Three of his friends travel to be with Job in order to "sympathize with him and comfort him" (v. 11). They don't just send comforting words and their sympathies to the family; they are there, physically present with Job. Job's actual siblings don't show up until it's time to celebrate, but his friends come during his darkest suffering and weep openly with him. Siblings in Christ should embrace these practices for one another when they are suffering.

But then things start to get weird. The friends say nothing to Job for seven days and seven nights. They just sit there. Many sermons and commentators teach that this silence is deeply compassionate, but Christopher Ash disagrees. While at first their silence may seem like an expression of solidarity, Ash points out that seven days of silence is just plain "eerie."[4] Seeing extreme suffering does provoke a reverent silence, so theirs may begin as a recognition of Job's pain and grief. That

---

3. I don't have the space here to cover an adequate theology of why we suffer or of God's sovereignty in our suffering. Many other books have done that well. See J. Todd Billings, *Rejoicing in Lament: Wrestling with Incurable Cancer and Life in Christ* (Grand Rapids: Brazos Press, 2015); Kelly M. Kapic, *Embodied Hope: A Theological Meditation on Pain and Suffering* (Downers Grove: IVP Academic, 2017); Christopher Ash, *Job: The Wisdom of the Cross* (Wheaton, IL: Crossway, 2014).

4. Ash, *Job*, 62.

is good. But seven days and nights of silence conveys a different message. Ash explains that "a seven-day silence symbolized mourning for the dead."[5] Job's friends fail in comforting Job and treat him as if he were dead.

This is the epitome of loneliness: Job's own wife tells him to curse his God and die, and his best friends treat him as if he already has. Ash refers to this tragic loneliness in suffering as "an unbridgeable gulf."[6] Job's friends are with him, yet he is "more deeply alone as he [sits] alongside them."[7] It's as if Job is completely dehumanized by his extreme pain. The friends' seven-day silence is the first clue that they aren't listening. You can't listen to a dead person.

But there is good news for Job and for us as well. As Job later confesses, his Redeemer lives, and we live on the other side of the resurrection (see Job 19:25). Ash teaches that Job's loneliness foreshadows the ultimate loneliness of our Savior on the cross. Christ was deserted by the friends he called brothers—friends who slept when he needed their comfort the most and left him during his brutal suffering on the cross. At least Job's friends wept with him. Jesus wept tears of blood alone. But even worse, in his darkest hour, he cried out from the cross, "My God, My God, why have You forsaken Me?" (Mark 15:34). And this too was for us. "There is a deep sense in which the lonely sufferings of Jesus Christ mean that no believer today is called to enter Job's loneliness in its full depth."[8]

> Suffering encloses a man in solitude. . . . Between Job and his friends an abyss was cleft. They regarded him with astonishment as a strange being. . . . But they could no longer get

5. Ash, 62.
6. Ash, 60.
7. Ash, 63.
8. Ash, 63.

205

to him. Only Jesus could cross this abyss, descend into the abyss of misery, plunge into the deepest hell.[9]

Suffering made up a vast part of Christ's work for our salvation, and this means that we are in solidarity with our Elder Brother when we suffer. "He had to be like his brothers and sisters in every way, so that he could become a merciful and faithful high priest in matters pertaining to God, to make atonement for the sins of the people. For since he himself has suffered when he was tempted, he is able to help those who are tempted" (Heb. 2:17–18 CSB). We don't choose suffering, but Christ chose to suffer for us. And when we are tempted to sin in our suffering, we can look to our Elder Brother who suffered in righteousness on our behalf. When we suffer, we are comforted to know that Jesus experienced suffering himself, that he has compassion on us, that he has won the victory over sin, that he will comfort us in our suffering now, and that he can keep us from being hardened by sin's deception while we wait for the end of our own sufferings (see Heb. 3:13). Suffering won't get the last word, and our brothers and sisters need to hear gospel truths as a reminder that our Elder Brother is our perfect High Priest who is merciful and faithful to the end. This is something that we can tell one another in our suffering.

In Christ, we have solidarity in suffering. We have solidarity with the one who experienced the greatest suffering, in the utmost solitude, so that we never will. And all of us who are in Christ can practice this solidarity by being present in one another's suffering. Sure, many times this is not a viable

---

9. Jean Daniélou, *Holy Pagans of the Old Testament*, trans. Felix Faber (London: Longmans, Green & Co., 1957), quoted in Nahum N. Glatzer, ed., *The Dimensions of Job: A Study and Selected Readings* (New York: Schocken Books, 1969), 109, quoted in Ash, 64.

option. Sending notes, meals, and even text messages to let someone know they are being prayed for and thought of is still encouraging. But we also do well to be present when we can—even to make sacrifices in order to be present. We can weep with those who weep. We can practice good listening and sympathizing and can genuinely comfort others by showing them that they are not in an unbridgeable gulf.

Training for Sibling Fruit

Suffering reveals what is in our hearts. The way we respond to suffering exposes what we really believe and what is most important to us. It causes us to face the *Who am I?* and *Where am I?* questions discussed earlier in this book. And, amazingly, suffering can yield fruit. Our hearts are disciplined and refined in suffering, whether we suffer as a direct result of sin or through a circumstance we have no control over. And our practices through suffering testify to this.

This is a painful process. In times of suffering, I have been instructed and comforted by Hebrews 12:11: "No chastening seems to be joyful for the present, but grievous; nevertheless, afterward it yields the peaceable fruit of righteousness to those who have been trained by it" (NKJV). I have particularly benefitted from Arthur Pink's commentary, which points out two words in this verse that I had never paid much attention to before.[10] The word *nevertheless* insinuates that every single one of us will suffer. But we aren't all affected in the same way. The word *afterward* is also revealing. What kind of person are we after affliction? "Have your past experiences hardened, soured, frozen you? Or have they softened, sweetened, mellowed you?

10. See Arthur Pink, *An Exposition of Hebrews* (repr., Grand Rapids: Baker, 2004), 978.

207

Has pride been subdued, self-pleasing been mortified, patience developed? How have afflictions, chastisements, left us? What does the 'afterward' reveal?"[11]

Suffering is never passive. We are to be "trained by it." In the original Greek, the word *trained* referred to gymnastic games, Pink explains, and it alludes to an athlete taking off his regular clothing. "Thus, this word in our text is almost parallel with the 'laying aside of every weight' in v.1. If afflictions cause us to be stripped of pride, sloth, selfishness, a revengeful spirit, then 'fruit' will be produced."[12] Because of his great love for us, God disciplines us through our suffering. He works to refine our hearts through sanctification. The rotten has to go. But first it needs to be revealed and dealt with. It is shocking to discover what's in our own hearts. I am motivated to train under suffering by the promise and goal of seeing the fruit of righteousness that our Lord will produce through it.

This isn't merely a personal exhortation. Hebrews 12:14–17 build on verse 11, charging us to look after our siblings when they suffer so that they are not tempted to sin. We aspire both to personal fruit and to sibling fruit in the covenant household of our Lord. Have you ever experienced the fruit of solidarity by suffering through the same experiences with someone? Since siblings share a family and a household, they have unique opportunities to go though trials together.

I experienced this in a powerful way in my own household. When I was fifteen, my siblings and I went through a trial that many children have to endure, even within the church. Our parents divorced. We had never thought that this would happen in our family. We thought that we had the perfect family! Friends, and even total strangers, would regularly compliment

11. Pink, 978.
12. Pink, 979.

us on how wonderful our family was. We went to church. We had family dinners. We took yearly vacations. We liked each other! Without getting into detail about what happened between my parents, I want to share a little of what happened between my siblings and me. We were devastated. We are even now. Some suffering remains. However, as our world fell apart, the three of us were trained through this suffering together. The immediate solidarity that came through our suffering still blooms and bursts with fruit to this day.

When divorce impacts children, they feel as though everything they thought they knew was a lie. Identity, faithfulness, love, faith, and security are all up for reevaluation. What do those words even mean? Are they possible? Our souls screamed for answers to questions that we weren't mature enough to articulate, even while our sense of loss drove us toward mature thinking. There was no turning back. We could only survive and move forward. But we were still siblings. That was one thing that did not change. We were in the same boat, and we were there for each other.

As the eldest sibling, I regret some of the ways that I handled my suffering. My acts of rebellion were terrible models to my brother and sister. We all had a lot of training to do, and so did our parents. Yet even our sin cannot hinder God's gracious working. He didn't overlook our sin; he exposed our own hearts to us. Through our suffering, he graciously, over time, revealed bitterness, pride, and a revengeful spirit in our hearts that needed to be stripped away.

By suffering together, my siblings and I came to know each other intimately. But the beautiful part is that we have also come to know our God more fully. Through the years, we have pointed one another to Christ, finding the answers to the questions that were so painful at one time. The Lord not only comforted and sustained us through our suffering but also produced the fruit of righteousness in each one of us, as well as a beautiful solidarity between us that continues to grow stronger. This is the training I am talking about.

Solidarity is based on a common union. By God's grace, my siblings and I discovered an even stronger union than the one our parents had once provided: our union in Christ. That is where we found the overflowing fruits of righteousness. All siblings in God's household have this union.

Christ is a much better Elder Brother than I was, or still am, as an older sister. But, by his grace, I am blessed to be my biological siblings' older sister, as well as both a younger and an older sister to my spiritual siblings. In God's household, we have solidarity with one another in suffering, which reveals our true hope for the fruit of righteousness.

Practicing Theologians

To practice something is to continually exercise what you already know in order to gain a certain target proficiency. It is easy to see how the practice of celebration points to our Christian expectation, while the practice of suffering seems more abstract. But when we continually celebrate and suffer together as siblings, we act as practicing theologians. The questions that my parents' divorce provoked in me are theological questions. And the answers to those questions are the confession of my hope.

The preacher to the Hebrews exhorts us as a church to persevere by holding fast to our confession of hope, together. "*Let us* hold fast the confession of our hope without wavering, for He who promised is faithful" (Heb. 10:23). We exercise these truths in our worship liturgy, as we sing both praises and songs of lament, as well as when we partake in corporate confession and absolution. And we exercise these truths in everyday life through our practices together. Both when celebratory occasions arise and when our siblings suffer, here's a question to consider: how does our response rehearse and strengthen what we believe to be true about the person and work of Jesus Christ? In our regular practices, we confess our beliefs together. Our actions reveal what we believe.

Sacred siblings are practicing theologians. We don't need to put on masks of righteousness before one another. Instead, we can be honest and can help one another strive for holiness in the good times and the bad. My brother and sister saw my sin when I was suffering from the divorce, and I saw theirs. Sin can also be revealed in the way that we celebrate. But our confession of hope, the good news of our salvation, tells us the truth about our condition. Since we have so great a Savior, we can confess our sins to one another.

Grace is confrontational. When we live under the reign of grace, we are confronted with the holiness of God and the evil of sin. We cannot remain in sin. We cannot pretend. Many siblings isolate themselves because their brothers and sisters are "unthinkably horrified when a real sinner is suddenly discovered among the righteous."[13] This shouldn't be. Whether we celebrate the blessings of God together or suffer together because of the curse of sin, we exercise our confession of hope—the ultimate blessing that Jesus is Lord.

Our solidarity comes from Christ's lordship. It is a true hope that we know. It isn't one that keeps us isolated, but one that moves us toward our brothers and sisters in communion. Training in these truths through everyday practices prepares us for that great expectation of holy communion with the triune God in the new heavens and the new earth, where celebration will ring eternal and suffering will never rise again.

13. Dietrich Bonhoeffer, *Life Together* (New York: Harper & Row, 1954), 110.

211

Sin will be vanquished, and our hearts will reveal only the fruits of righteousness.

Discussion Questions

1. Have you experienced solidarity with biological siblings? How is that different from your other friendships? Do you have that kind of solidarity with your brothers and sisters in Christ?
2. How can sharing in the practices of celebration and suffering be good practice in properly orienting our sibling affection and solidarity? How would our earlier teaching on Romans 11:36 guide us here?
3. Do you find it difficult to celebrate someone else's success? Do you tend to isolate yourself from your friends when they are going through suffering? What spiritual fruit are you missing out on, for both yourself and your friends, because of this?

13

Model Affectionate,
Appropriate Relationships
to the Watching World

In the first chapter, we asked, "Who am I?" Do people buy the image that we offer them? Now, in this final chapter, it's time to ask, "Who are we, the church?" Do people really know us, or do they just see the image that we want them to see? What do unbelievers know about the church, and what do we want them to believe? Are these the same thing? What is the reputation of God's family?

We know what we want people to believe about God, but it's a lot tougher for us to be his image bearers. What does the quality of our life together tell outsiders to the faith? Do our relationships and our love for one another match up with our confession of hope? Is our church household one that "faithfully reflects God's purposes as well as the reality of current human existence—including dignity and struggle, universality and particularity, relationality and personal identity, all understood within the framework of love and communion"?[1]

Can men and women be friends? By now, that question may be nearly forgotten! Even unbelievers wrestle with this issue and long to see it worked out. Spiritual friendship with those of the same or the opposite sex is true, rich, and beautiful. But it's also hard sometimes.

It's easy to excuse ourselves or to reduce the richness of the communion to which we are called. Yes, the church is made up of redeemed sinners. We are not in our glorified states yet, and we can be honest about that. We want the world to know that we are grateful for redemption and that we hate sin. And it's easy to make hard-and-fast rules to help us avoid sin in our friendships, but these can limit our capacity for growth. This is not the communion that we are called to, and unbelievers see right through it. They're not buying it. Where's the redemption? What are we being redeemed to?

Redemption is about making something holy, set apart for the worship of God—nothing less. Our great news is that we have been made holy in Christ, and we get to enjoy communion with our holy God. Holy people are called to holy relationships, and our communion with the triune God makes us outgoing in our love for others.

Are We Selling a Lie?

What does it tell the world when church leaders send the same message as Billy Crystal—and when the church respects them for it? For Billy Crystal's character, Harry Burns, and for many in the church, the "sex part" gets in the way of friendship

---

1. Kelly M. Kapic, "Anthropology," from *Christian Dogmatics: Reformed Theology for the Church Catholic*, ed. Michael Allen and Scott R. Swain (Grand Rapids: Baker Academic, 2016), 166.

between men and women. There are important differences between the two views, of course. Burns teaches that a woman can *never* really have guy friends. The Christian equivalent suggests that men should avoid women as threats to marriage, purity, and the reputations of godly leaders. Sure, women are okay as acquaintances in social settings, but friendship is too far.

Is this really all there is? Is our greatest hope for intimacy and communion to be found only in a marriage so fragile that giving someone else a car ride can ruin it? Do Christian marriages, which were designed for this lifetime only, display Christ's love for his church to outsiders if we put this kind of pressure on one another?

If the church can't answer the question of friendship between men and women, why would unbelievers want us to tell them about holy communion with God? Is the Lord really good, or is he cruel? Does God call us to "fervently love one another from the heart" because we have been born again "through the living and enduring word of God" (1 Peter 1:22–23) while at the same time giving us sexual urges that prevent us from sharing lunch in the middle of the day or from offering a convenient ride to someone? If we can't be trusted to have enough integrity to show one another common decency, then our souls are far from purified, and we certainly can't have a sincere or fervent love for one another.

But we, who "have tasted that the Lord is good" (1 Peter 2:3 csb), have been called "out of darkness into His marvelous light" (1 Peter 2:9). We "once were not a people, but now [we] are the people of God" (v. 10). This is what we want the world to see, right? This is the truth, right? In that case, the apostle Peter urges us as God's people who are living in the fallen world to "abstain from fleshly lusts which wage war against the soul" (v. 11) and to keep our behavior excellent in front of the watching world so that they will look at us in wonder and not be able to keep themselves from glorifying God (see v. 12). This is the bottom line! To reiterate, we claim to have a different allegiance, a different agency and purpose, and a different love than the world offers. Outsiders should sense that they really are on the outside of holiness and godly love when they see this in action. They should see that we aren't just talking talk and building a false image. The values of the world should be contrasted with the values of God's people *in our relationships*. They are looking for this.

Contagious Sibling Love

And we have what the world is looking for. What I have just described is a supernatural love that flows only when we are in a certain family—God's family. God has made us new creatures in Christ and given us his Holy Spirit. So we have this love, and God calls us to depend on the one who gives it, recognizing that it flows from him, through him, and back to him. We claim that we have this, and outsiders to the faith look for evidence.

Additionally, outsiders are blessed by our "inside" sibling love for one another. I advise women to marry men who grew up in a household with sisters—those men have already learned about very real distinctions between the sexes that cannot easily be reduced to stereotypes. Sure, men don't need to have biological sisters in order to relate well to women, and the mother-son relationship is another important exposure to femininity. But having sisters helps. It's a blessing. And that sibling solidarity that we grow in affects our relationships outside our households.

I've been interacting with a brother for most of my life. I know how to relate to guys. And having a loving brother helped me to understand how I should be treated by a man—not only in a marriage but in friendships as well. My brother and I would never think of reducing each other to sexual objects. We learned to treat each other with dignity. That doesn't mean that we didn't quarrel or act immature toward each other but that we began to learn about sibling solidarity through even our not-so-shining moments. Bad behavior was never tolerated. Playfulness was encouraged, and it was never confused with flirting because we expressed our sexuality in our brotherhood and sisterhood, not in eroticism. We knew that we had a responsibility toward each other—the bonus was that we enjoyed each other's presence. We still do.

Outsiders notice the love that all my siblings and I have for one another. We obviously care deeply for one another, seek one another's holiness, and just plain enjoy being together. But our sibling love doesn't hinder our friendships with those who aren't related to us. It has helped us to love others well too. We've learned a lot about friendship together.

Likewise, our sibling relationships in God's household help us to love our unbelieving friends well. Our shared practices continue outside the church doors. In all friendships, as Christine Pohl pointed out, we practice truthfulness, hospitality, making and keeping promises, table fellowship, gratitude, promoting holiness, celebrating and suffering together, discernment, and forgiveness. The conditioning that we get from these practices in God's household equips us well in all our relationships. Our unbelieving friends will share many of these practices with us, though not all. Some will seem strange, like the practice of keeping the Sabbath in worship. But this benefits them as well. It teaches them that the household we are a part of is not of this world. It teaches them that there is a holy God who calls us to worship. It teaches them that we rest in Christ before we are called back into the world.

As we participate in regular practices in our friendships,

we live with integrity toward our friends. And it is contagious. Who doesn't appreciate a good friend?

Four Foundations

My case for Christian friendship between the sexes has involved four key theological elements. While unbelievers won't articulate it this way, what they notice in Christian friendship displays what we believe about our anthropology, eschatology, Christology, and ecclesiology.

Anthropology

What do outsiders notice about what matters to us? Do they see that we don't view each other reductively because we know *that the whole person matters*? Do they see that we care about the mind, body, and soul of all ages, races, and sexes?

Unbelievers should also notice that *agency and purpose matter* to us. The very fact that we are purposeful in our friendships shows that we see ourselves created for relationship, both with our triune God and with one another, and that God has given us the faculties to have these relationships. They will see that our redemption gives us the capacity to truly do good to one another in a way that glorifies God.

Our Christian friendships model that *relational growth matters*. This distinguishes humanity from the rest of creation. As we grow in our knowledge of and communion with our Lord, this overflows into abundant, rightly ordered love for one another. As we grow, our relationships grow. We work toward this rather than implementing hard-and-fast rules that stunt growth.

We exercise wisdom and discernment, because we know that *sin matters*. Sin is evil. It separates us from God. He calls us to choose affliction over sin. And we desperately need the

Son's work on our behalf for communion with God and the continuing work of his Holy Spirit for sanctification. We promote one another's holiness in Christian love.

In our friendships, unbelievers see that *representation and solidarity matter*. In our friendships, outsiders behold God's people participating in the Father's great love for his Son through his Spirit. What a beautiful picture! What a wonder for them to notice formerly rebellious, sinful creatures restored into goodness. They will notice that God's redeemed have renewed minds that affect the way we live with one another.

Eschatology

Outsiders notice a driving force in our relationships. As new creations, we are headed for eternal life with our triune God and one another in the new heavens and the new earth. This world is not all there is. Rather than surrendering our sexuality to stereotypical gender tropes, we look to how our sexuality will be manifested in the new creation. We look backward to our created purpose, the fall, and redemption, and we look forward to resurrected bodies.

In the future, when we are all Christ's bride, we will not be given in marriage to one another, but we will relate to one another in perfect representation of the image of God. What will manhood and womanhood look like then? We value our marriages here—they showcase the gospel, give us companionship, and bring the potential for offspring—but we also value singlehood in the community of the faith. Singlehood shouldn't mean isolation from intimacy. In all relationships, our affections should be rightly oriented toward godly expression.

Christology

The way we relate to one another is rooted in our relationship with our Elder Brother, Jesus Christ. He is the keeper of our souls, the ultimate priest who brings us into communion with the Father through the Spirit. We are adopted into God's family as sons in the Son and are sacred siblings to one another. This adoption includes intimacy with our Brother, access to the Father, and the full inheritance of the resurrected Christ. Our sibling solidarity reflects our solidarity in Christ. Unbelievers should see Christ in our relationships with one another and the sibling love that we have as a result.

Ecclesiology

How do outsiders view church? What do our relationships tell them about it? Do they see a place where we just go to hear a sermon and sing a few songs, or do they notice a household dynamic? What does the household look like? Is there order? Is there affection? Is there solidarity, harmony, and unity? Is there love? How do God's people receive Christ and all his benefits? The world wants to know! Many will be brought into the family, and many will reject God's call, but let's give them an accurate representation of our status in God's household.

One second-century outsider to the faith, Lucian of Samosata, despised Christianity but still noted the special relationships of the people in God's household and the extraordinary way in which Christians cared for their own.

> The poor wretches have convinced themselves, first and foremost, that they are going to be immortal and live for all time, in consequence of which they despise death and even willingly give themselves into custody, most of them. Furthermore, their first lawgiver persuaded them that they are all brothers of one another after they have transgressed once for all by denying the Greek gods and by worshipping that crucified sophist himself and living under his laws.[2]

2. Lucian, *The Passing of Peregrinus*, ed. Thomas E. Page, trans. Austin M. Harmon,

Lucian couldn't get over how Christians treated one another favorably, as one does a family member. They even went out of their way to comfort prisoners who professed the faith, bringing them elaborate meals and books and even bribing the prison guards so they could provide company and companionship. He "was widely traveled in the East and was, therefore, familiar with Christian practices in Palestine, Asia, and Egypt. His background—along with his obvious lack of sympathy for the Jesus movement—makes him a reliable witness to early Christian social solidarity."[3] Lucian knew what he was rejecting. He knew because he observed people who believed they were in God's family, who cared for the mind, body, and soul of others, who believed they were headed for eternal life in a new creation, who hated and rejected sin, and who loved one another selflessly in accordance with their unity in a Savior—a man who claimed to be God. Lucian saw an ordered household code and sibling solidarity. It is truly amazing to see this in the screed of an unbeliever! He thought he was cursing God, but he was in fact glorifying his work.

Free to Be Fervent and Not a Pervert

Is friendship cheap? Is it easily come by? The world views friendship as disposable. At the same time, it takes language that used to be associated with friendship and reserves it for romantic love. Meanwhile, in Christian circles, some are uncomfortable with having their own Facebook "friends." Some married couples share an account, or do not "friend" members of the opposite sex, in order to avoid sin. Friendship is losing all its meaning.

---

vol. 5 (Cambridge: Harvard University Press, 1936), 13, quoted in Joseph H. Hellerman, *The Ancient Church as Family* (Minneapolis: Fortress Press, 2001), 128.

3. Hellerman, *The Ancient Church as Family*, 128.

The late-nineteenth-century work of Richard von Krafft-Ebing, Albert Moll, and Sigmund Freud marked the shift toward sexualizing all affectionate language.

> Following the biological argument of Charles Darwin, Krafft-Ebing believed that self-preservation and sexual gratification were fundamental human instincts. Moll also stressed that the sexual instinct was a basic, irrational, complicated and very powerful drive that was difficult to suppress. . . . For Krafft-Ebing and Moll, love, as a social bond, was inherently sexual.[4]

Their work led to the Harry Burns mentality: affection is only a means to sex. Now, even with friends of the same sex, we shy away from affection. No self-respecting man today would utter to his best bud, "I am distressed for you, my brother Jonathan; you have been very pleasant to me. Your love to me was more wonderful than the love of women," much less kiss him and weep together with him (2 Sam. 1:26; see also 1 Sam. 20:41). They would be accused of homosexuality—because it's got to be about sex, right?

Likewise, we have taken a section from Scripture about sibling love in God's household and used it for marriage ceremonies:

> Love is patient, love is kind and is not jealous; love does not brag and is not arrogant, does not act unbecomingly; it does not seek its own, is not provoked, does not take into account a wrong suffered, does not rejoice in unrighteousness, but rejoices with the truth; bears all things,

---

4. Harry Oosterhuis, "Sexual Modernity in the Works of Richard von Krafft-Ebing and Albert Moll," *Medical History* 56, no. 2 (April 2012), available online at https://www.ncbi.nlm.nih.gov/pmc/articles/PMC3381524/.

believes all things, hopes all things, endures all things. (1 Cor. 13:4–7)

Why do we reserve this teaching for marriage when Paul used it to describe the way that brothers and sisters in the Lord are to worshipfully share our gifts in his household?

Ruth makes a strong covenant with her mother-in-law Naomi after the death of her husband, Naomi's son: "Do not urge me to leave you or turn back from following you; for where you go, I will go, and where you lodge, I will lodge. Your people shall be my people, and your God, my God" (Ruth 1:16). Wait a minute—these are women from ancient history. I thought they were incapable of virtuous friendship. Snark aside, do we see fervent love and commitment like this in our friendships today?

Sadly, even if we wanted to express affection and obligation like this to our friends, it would be viewed as perverted—or, at the very least, hard to trust. Where will the world see godly friendships that showcase the freedom to love well?

We Can Be Friends!

Many like to answer the question about friendship between the sexes in the negative because they have anecdotal examples of when it has gone wrong. These are powerful warnings indeed. But we have examples from church history that showcase a beautiful answer in the positive. Before our culture became so sexualized, plenty of Christians modeled intimate coed friendships.

In a chapter cataloguing complementary spiritual friendships between men and women in Roman Catholic history, Paul Conner highlights passionate friendships between Blessed Jordan of Saxony and Diana d'Andalo, St. Catherine of Siena and Blessed Raymond of Capua, St. Teresa of Avila and Father Gerome Gracian, and St. Francis de Sales and Jane de Chantal.[5] Their correspondences were testaments to their special friendships and were filled with intimate expressions of affection for each other.

Conner particularly showcases St. Catherine of Siena's and St. Teresa of Avila's thoughts on friendships between the sexes. "They hold that for consecrated men and women with the right disposition of faith, prudence, and zeal for the other virtues . . . human friendship can be a providential means for growth in friendship with God."[6] These men and women lived this truth out in their friendships with passionate fervor and chastity.

Pastors during the Reformation didn't have any hang-ups about engaging in endearing friendships with women either. That stood out to me as I was reading about French princess and Italian duchess, Renée of France.

> A major element in Renée's life is her correspondence with French Reformer, John Calvin, which continues for most of her life and opens a window on less familiar aspects of his soul. Of all his correspondence with women, his letters to Renée are unique, revealing a close bond of friendship. Calvin often feels free to reveal his struggles to her in a way he would not do with others, and she talks openly and trustingly about her puzzlement, fear, and exasperation.[7]

Calvin's death ended twenty-seven years of correspondence between the two—"the longest and most pastoral

5. See Paul M. Conner, *Celibate Love* (Huntington, IN: Our Sunday Visitor, 1979), 49–96.
6. Conner, 95.
7. Simonetta Carr, *Renée of France*, Bitesize Biographies (Grand Rapids: Evangelical Press, 2013), 14.

correspondence the Reformer ever kept with a noblewoman."[8] And to think that he didn't even cc his wife in on these letters! Disgraceful! . . . unless, of course, platonic friends actually do exist.

Renée was more than an auxiliary support to men. Calvin didn't reduce her to her one role as the duke's wife. She was a sister in Christ with a soul and a mind of her own. She wasn't even an easy friend, but one who asked hard questions, openly disagreed, and took risks. They were friends who sharpened each other, which produced fruit that lasted longer than their lives on this earth.

Perhaps writer and activist Hannah More lived at the end of the time when an honored Christian woman could enjoy affectionate friendship with a man and neither of them lose their reputation for it. Renowned literary giant Samuel Johnson enjoyed a close friendship with her. They "developed an immediate and strong affection for each other,"[9] which involved a vigorous intellectual and creative bond as well as much laughter and teasing.[10] Using terms of affection toward Hannah such as *love* and *dearest* were not strikes against Samuel's character.[11]

Hannah also enjoyed a close friendship with one of the most famous actors of the time—a married man, David Garrick. His mentor role with her is described as blossoming into a familial bond that both David and his wife shared with Hannah.[12] "The friendship between Garrick and More was so deep and so well known that More, along with his widow, received offers and letters of condolence" after his

---

8. Carr, 107.

9. Karen Swallow Prior, *Fierce Convictions: The Extraordinary Life of Hannah More; Poet, Reformer, Abolitionist* (Nashville: Nelson Books, 2014), 58.

10. See Prior, 58–63.

11. See Prior, 59.

12. See Prior, 68.

death.[13] More also enjoyed endearing friendships with John Newton and William Wilberforce. "More's relationship with Wilberforce would prove to be—apart from those with her sisters—one of the longest lasting and dearest of her life. Their friendship lasted uninterrupted for forty-seven years. They died within weeks of each other."[14]

We know about these success stories of affectionate friendships because of the letters they left behind. We don't need to speculate about the nature of their relationships, because we see actual proof of the intimacy and platonic nature of their friendships in their writing. We see that Christ was surely the focus and the glory of their relationships. And these friendships blessed the world, leaving long-lasting fruit after their deaths.

Through their unapologetic correspondences when they were absent from each other, we learn that not all intimacy is shameful. Perhaps the Christ-centered intimacy in these letters is a small glimpse into the sibling relationships that we will enjoy without sin for eternity.

Distinction without Reduction

The world flattens the sexes by stereotyping feminine and masculine traits. But the truth is that men also have what we call feminine traits and that women also have what we call masculine traits. Yet when a man naturally exercises a so-called feminine trait, he does so differently from a woman, and vice versa. Everyone is unique in our combination of traits, and our relationships with the other sex complement what we lack. We weren't created to exist independently, and rich friendships need to extend beyond same-sex boundaries.

13. Prior, 71.
14. Prior, 116.

Masculine-feminine friendship can be the preeminent form of true friendship. At first sight it may seem that a man and a woman are not similar enough for the basic requirement of friendship. Two men or two women would seem more similar. The reality of complementary between the sexes, however, shows that two halves of the human whole may be more "alike" than any two incomplete halves of the same sex.[15]

Man and woman are made in the image of God, so we should long for complementarity in our friendships as we seek God above all things. What do Christians desire for themselves and all others? We long to behold the ultimate blessedness of God! And so we want to see our friends as God sees them, and we want to reflect Christ to them. We long to gaze on the beauty of God, and, as we seek that in others, we get a taste of that beauty.[16] So we are to point others to Christ, not to ourselves—although we hope that our friends see a reflection of Christ's blessedness in us.

Friends are blessings of God. They reflect Christ in unique ways, giving us a deeper knowledge of him and therefore giving us a taste of that "'nearness by resemblance' to Heaven itself where the very multitude of the blessed (which no man can number) increases the fruition which each has of God."[17] "Without friends, who would want to live?"[18]

In a world that equates loving with consuming and

15. Conner, *Celibate Love*, 109.

16. See Nathan Lefler, *Theologizing Friendship: How Amicitia in the Thought of Aelred and Aquinas Inscribes the Scholastic Turn* (Eugene, OR: Pickwick Publications, 2014), 95.

17. C. S. Lewis, *The Four Loves* (1960; repr., New York: Harcourt Brace, 1991), 62.

18. See Jean-Pierre Torrell, *Saint Thomas Aquinas*, vol. 2, *Spiritual Master*, trans. Robert Royal (Washington, D.C.: The Catholic University of America Press, 2003), chap. 12.

affection with erotica, many are so confused. Men are trying to *become* women, and vice versa. One message says that sexuality is fluid and there are no real distinctions between the sexes, and another reduces the sexes to a means of physical gratification. Those who struggle with same-sex attraction are wrestling with how it affects their identity, with the way others will relate to them, and with how to rightly orient their affections. With all of the sexual brokenness, sin, and confusion in the world, we need to learn to be good friends.

"Eros, like Dionysus, is a great and dangerous god."[19] He cares nothing for friendship. He cares nothing for affections. And he hates the beauty of holiness. But we know differently. Our identity is in Christ! We are *becoming* like him! And affections that are oriented toward the triune God can't help but reap the fruit of his blessedness. In the blessing of godly friendship, the world sees rich communion that generously promotes our friends in our true identities. Those who struggle with same-sex attraction and want to honor God by not committing sexual sin have a difficult time making friends in a church that follows the world in overly sexualizing people. They need to hear and be encouraged by these truths. So do we, as living in the light of these truths illustrates *dignity and struggle, rationality and personal identity*. All of us together can live in the truth that our sexuality isn't reduced to sexual urges or stereotypical roles.

Additionally, godly friendship recognizes and appreciates distinction between, and even within, the sexes. Virtuous friendships, in which we aim for the good of both our friends and ourselves, grow when we both share certain qualities and also have different qualities to offer and receive. "Since men

---

19. Camille Paglia, *Sex, Art, and American Culture: Essays* (New York: Vintage Books, 1992), 30.

and women are a mixture on all levels of masculinity and femininity, it becomes clear how they can love each other . . . based respectively on the actual likenesses they share and the mutual need for perfection they offer each other."[20] All of us have something to offer in friendship, and none of us is without need. Femininity helps to develop masculinity, and vice versa—but not when we reduce it to stereotypes or imposed cultural roles.

Outsiders are watching Christian relationships. Do they see a difference in God's people? Even today, I saw the question of whether men and women can be friends posed once again on social media—by a Christian. And once again in the comments I see a theme: we don't understand what friendship really is. We know that it matters, but we don't know why. *Can men and women be friends?* It's the wrong question. How could we even ask such a question if we understood the meaning of friendship?

Are we opposed to friendship? No—we are opposed to sin, and we are *for* holiness. And for this reason, men and women are called to be more than friends. We are called to Christ, in whom we become brothers and sisters. As the saying goes, blood runs thicker than water.

> There is a fountain filled with blood,
> Drawn from Immanuel's veins;
> And sinners plunged beneath that flood,
> Lose all their guilty stains:
>
> . . . .
>
> E'er since by faith I saw the stream
> Thy flowing wounds supply,

20. Conner, *Celibate Love*, 110.

Redeeming love has been my theme,
And shall be till I die.[21]

Discussion Questions

1. In this chapter I said that the values of the world should be contrasted with the values of God's people *in our relationships*. What does the quality of your relationships show about what you value? What does the quality of your friendships show about your view of anthropology, eschatology, Christology, and ecclesiology?
2. How does our status as brothers and sisters uphold distinction between the sexes, without reduction, to a world that is searching for answers about sexuality?
3. Think about the anecdotal examples in your life of men and women who have fallen into sexual sin. How have they cheapened both friendship and marriage? How do the examples given in this chapter uphold true friendship, purity, and Christian marriage?

21. William Cowper, "There Is a Fountain Filled with Blood," 1772.

CONCLUSION

What Now?

Well, you've read my case for friendship between the sexes. Now what? What do I hope you will do, now that you've invested this time into the question?

Please read what I've said with Christian discernment, charity, and maturity. I am not calling for some kind of new movement within the church in which men and women begin flaunting their friendships. I want nothing to do with that. We don't need a movement. We do need real friends.

I'm not calling for us all to expect the type of friendships that Hannah More had with William Wilberforce or that John Calvin had with Renée of France. Those were special blessings that we can be grateful to have as an example, and any of us would indeed be thankful for such a gift of faithful friendship.

But, like them, we should not settle for a cheapened view of friendship or purity. That is easy to do in our culture, with the disembodied, noncommittal friendships that are encouraged on social media sites, the over-sexualization of men and women, and the stereotypical gender tropes that are touted even in our own evangelical circles. No, the church should be the very place that reveals the deficiency of these frames of reference. Friendship is genuine, embodied, and pure.

I am simply asking you to *be* a friend, because friendship is something you do. It isn't about getting friends. It isn't about you. And it isn't an excuse to be inappropriate. Friends don't do that. But it is not only inappropriate to turn a friendship into a forbidden romance; it is just as inappropriate to withhold a friendly act such as offering a ride to a person in need, engaging in normal work practices, or being an advocate in other ways during your everyday situations. That sends just as much of a reductive message. Be a friend and promote holiness in everyone whom you encounter and whom God trusts to your care. Look at one another through the eyes of Christ.

There is a reason we should be able to perform these simple acts of friendship. And that points to the more crucial takeaway point of my book. This is what I want for us now: the church should be the very place where the world sees genuine friendship, no matter what sex you are. No matter what race you are. No matter what your social status is. This is where the world should be able to look and see what friendship is and how you do it. And when men and women view and treat one another as holistic people made in the image of God who are investing in something more than the here and now, they show that friendship points to something more permanent than what this world offers. Friendship looks beyond our finitude to what we expect to be in eternity. Friendship points to our truest friend and advocate, Jesus Christ. And he cannot be cheapened. Furthermore, friendship points to the mission of our triune God: eternal communion with his people. Is your church a picture of this?

Because of these truths, we should also be pursuing lasting, godly friendships. The quality of our relationships should match our confession of hope. Therefore, being friendly also calls for wisdom and discernment. We should not invest the bulk of our time into those who wallow in cheap friendship. And a funny thing happens when you refuse to settle. As we become good friends to others, we find good friends. What a beautiful gift friendship is! What a gracious God we have, who can show us beauty even as we work through the curse of sin that we still live under in this lifetime.

Friendship gives a glimpse of God's blessedness, a glimpse of his glory. Even in our pain, toil, and tiredness, we can see the hope of eternity in friendship. That helps us to hold on for that Great Day when we will behold our God in all his glory, when all sin will be judged, all dross will be burned, all suffering will be ended, and friendship will remain.

APPENDIX

Siblings in Scripture

Sibling relationships saturate Scripture, as God has always purposed his covenants with his people to extend to their offspring. I would have to write another whole book to cover all the siblings in Scripture.

Three different sets of siblings stand out to me in God's Word, illustrating both the blessings of siblingship and the rivalry that we still have to battle before Christ's return. Although Job's children do not play a lead role in his story, accounts of siblings bookend it. Elsewhere in the Old Testament, two brothers and a sister play an important role in the history of redemption, and in the New Testament two sisters and a brother have a special relationship with our Redeemer.

What Job Teaches Us About Siblings

In the book of Job, Scripture gives us a fascinating glimpse of a household in the patriarchal world—maybe longer ago than 1500 BC. Right away we are told that Job was "blameless,

Appendix

upright, fearing God and turning away from evil" (Job 1:1). Abraham was called out from a pagan family, but Job knew, loved, and obeyed God. He knew and worshipped God before Israel's enslavement, exile, and deliverance, before the law was given and the priesthood instituted.

The very next thing we learn about Job is that he was blessed with seven sons and three daughters (see v. 2). Explaining that the number seven denotes completeness and therefore seven sons is akin to a complete blessing, Christopher Ash highlights that Ruth is described as a greater blessing to her mother-in-law, Naomi, than seven sons (see Ruth 4:15) and that Hannah's great prayer praising the "gospel reversals of God" proclaims, "Even the barren gives birth to seven" (1 Sam. 2:5). "What more could a man want than seven sons!" Ash asks. "Well, I guess some daughters as well. And three is a good number. And seven plus three equals ten, which is also a good number. They are all good numbers and speak of an ideal family."[1]

So Job has an ideal family full of sons and daughters. Maybe we could say that three daughters can accomplish what it would take seven sons to do, but I digress. Joking aside, we quickly get a glimpse into the households of the brothers and the family dynamic:

> His sons used to go and hold a feast in the house of each one on his day, and they would send and invite their three sisters to eat and drink with them. When the days of feasting had completed their cycle, Job would send and consecrate them, rising up early in the morning and offering burnt offerings according to the number of them all; for Job said, "Perhaps my sons have sinned and cursed God in their hearts." Thus Job did continually. (vv. 4–5)

1. Christopher Ash, *Job: The Wisdom of the Cross* (Wheaton: Crossway, 2014), 33.

236

Here we have a lovely description of the hosting brother inviting all his siblings for quite a feast. From this description, it
looks like they truly enjoyed one another's presence and lav-
ishly celebrated each sibling's life. Harmony and unity between
siblings was upheld, and this was good.

Although Job was blessed to have adult children who loved
one another, he cared about the inner man and was sensitive
to the depravity in their hearts. Even though there's no indica-
tion of any outward sin during their feasts, Job called on his
children, and particularly his sons, first thing the next morning and made a burnt offering to the Lord for each of them in
case they had sinned against God in their hearts. Job desired
complete holiness before the Lord for his whole family. Now
that's a beautiful picture of a household.

But we know the story of Job. With God's permission,
Satan destroys Job's wealth, his entire household except for
his wife, and even his health. Satan cannot destroy Job's righteousness, because Job's righteousness is not in himself—he
is a man of faith. We can learn a lot in this book about God,
man, faith, suffering, friends, providence, and our Redeemer.
But I find it interesting that the beginning and ending of the
book highlight Job's blessings by focusing on his children's
households. When God restores Job, some new brothers and
sisters enter the scene: Job's. They come to feast with him in
his home and to bring him gifts and consolation. Next we learn
that Job is restored with the blessings of another seven sons
and three daughters.

In the beginning of Job, the focus is on the seven sons.
The sons are prominent—the hosts of the feasts and perhaps
the only children summoned in the sacrificial offerings. But by
the end of the story, there's an interesting twist. In the account
of Job's restoration, the focus is on the daughters:

He had seven sons and three daughters. He named the first Jemimah, and the second Keziah, and the third Keren-happuch. In all the land no women were found so fair as Job's daughters; and their father gave them inheritance among their brothers. (42:13–15)

We learn the daughters' names but not the sons'. Their beauty is renowned. And, unlike most daughters in this patriarchal time, Job's daughters receive an inheritance among their brothers.

What is the significance of this change in emphasis? We shouldn't make too much of it, pitting one sex against the other. But in this restoration we see the beauty of femininity, equality, and harmony in the household. This is a big deal at a time when women were associated with shame and had little to no rights. This picture of harmony and eschatological restoration elevates what was considered the weaker sex. Mark Jones likes to think of this description of Job's daughters as a picture of our three theological virtues.

Faith, hope, and love have been referred to as the three divine sisters. I like to think of them as three beautiful sisters (like Job's daughters), joined hand in hand, dancing around in a circle together. Eventually, the one sister, love, separates from faith and hope and forever dances alone, while faith and hope vanish from the scene. That picture may appear odd until we realize that faith and hope were there to help love on her way until she was mature enough to be alone. For she exists as the greatest of the sisters and deserves the preeminence, just as Christ remains the greatest of the sons of men and deserves the same.[2]

2. Mark Jones, *Faith. Hope. Love.: The Christ-Centered Way to Grow in Grace* (Wheaton, IL: Crossway, 2017), 13–14.

Perhaps their mention does point to this theological reality for the church, God's household. But we can definitely say that we see the language of sisterhood being used to describe such beauty, blessing, harmony, and hope. That is encouraging.

Two Brothers and a Sister

Miriam, Aaron, and Moses show us a lot about sibling love and devoted service to the Lord. Big sister Miriam assists her mother when they desperately lean on faith in God and place three-month-old Moses in a basket on the Nile River. Miriam watches as the pharaoh's daughter spots the baby and has pity on him. She then offers to find someone to nurse the baby, and, of course, she brings their mother to Pharaoh's daughter, who will now pay her to nurse her own son until he is weaned (see Ex. 2:1–10).

Later, when God calls Moses to lead his people out of Egypt, he graciously reunites him with his older brother, Aaron, who helps to speak to his people on his behalf (see Ex. 4:1–17). How wonderful it must have been for these two brothers to be there for each other, serving together with faith, trepidation, and excitement! This is a strong illustration of brotherly solidarity in adulthood, even though these brothers were not even raised together.

We don't find Miriam in the text again until after the confrontations with Pharaoh, the plagues, and the Jews' great escape from Egypt through the parting of the Red Sea. Then Miriam the prophetess, tambourine in hand, leads the women in singing a response to Moses' song of praise to the Lord (see Ex. 15:20–21). This is beautiful—brother and sister leading the Israelites in praise together for all that the Lord has done!

But it's not all sunshine and roses for these siblings. Rivalry enters in. Moses' first wife, Zipporah, presumably dies, and he marries a Cushite woman with darker skin. Aaron and Miriam speak out. Maybe they don't like the fact that he has remarried, but either way their response is racist. *A Cushite woman, Moses? Really?* Along with their racism, jealousy also creeps in. *Who does Moses think he is? Does he have more authority than we do? Hasn't God also used us as prophet and priest?* "'Has the Lord indeed spoken only through Moses? Has He not spoken through us as well?'" (Num. 12:2).

The Lord immediately deals with this sin, calling all three to the tent of meeting. He vindicates Moses and his special call on him, and judgment falls on Miriam: leprosy (see Num. 12:1–10). After judging the color of Moses' wife's skin, Miriam's skin becomes much whiter than she would like! "In his judgment of Miriam, God is saying, 'Do you think your lighter skin makes you better than the woman Moses married? You want to be white? I'll give you white.'"[3]

But Aaron pleads with Moses for mercy, and Moses intercedes for his siblings to the Lord, crying out, "O God, heal her, I pray!" (v. 13). God heals Miriam, who suffers the softer consequence of being removed from the camp for one week.

In Aaron, Miriam, and Moses, we see a close relationship that lasts until death. We see their harmony and honor for one another, which promotes unity. We also see the damage that resulted when they failed to be unified, followed by immediate restoration. These siblings were blessings to one another as they worked to further the mission of God for the redemption of his people. None of them got to enter the Promised Land. In fact, Numbers 20 is a pretty depressing chapter that includes the deaths of Miriam and Aaron, as well as Moses' fatal sin. But God was faithful to his promise. Their ultimate hope was in a better land that is eternal.

3. James Montgomery Boice, *The Life of Moses: God's First Deliverer of Israel* (Phillipsburg, NJ: P&R, 2018), 303.

Two Sisters and a Brother

I always glean new things when I look at the relationship that siblings Martha, Mary, and Lazarus had with Jesus. This family fascinates me. No spouses are mentioned, and we are first introduced to the sisters of this sibling trio (see Luke 10:38–42). We don't see Mary and Martha as daughters, wives, or mothers—just as sisters living together.

Martha pursues the Christ, inviting him to their home, and Jesus accepts an invitation to the household of these two women. Martha is probably hoping to spend time in his presence, but Mary isn't merely enjoying his presence—she is sitting at his feet like a disciple learning from a rabbi. It's understandable that Martha feels cheated. A special guest deserves special treatment, but Mary is the one really benefitting here. She is being taught by Jesus! In fact, as Jesus shows, the highest calling for both of these women is to be his disciples.

The sisters get the chance to show Jesus that they've been listening. When their brother is near death, they send for Jesus, saying, "Lord, behold, he whom You love is sick" (John 11:3). That makes me wonder about the bond that they had. As he talks with the disciples, Jesus refers to Lazarus as their friend (see v. 11)—someone they all care about. But he waits for Lazarus to die so that they all may believe.

Of course, the sisters question his delay and grieve their brother's death. After Lazarus has been in the tomb for four days, the sisters get word that Jesus is a couple of miles away. Martha doesn't wait. Once again, she pursues Jesus. And, when she meets him, Martha says what's on her mind.

The interaction is one of great intimacy and vulnerability (see vv. 21–27), in which Jesus cuts right to the chase. Grieving, despairing, and confused by his actions, Martha confronts Jesus, and he confronts her. They stand eye-to-eye. Jesus lays out the truth about who he is and asks, "Do you believe this?" (v. 26). Martha knows Jesus: "I have believed that You are the Christ, the Son of God, even He who comes into the world" (v. 27). This is the most important thing.

Jesus then calls for Mary, and she passionately throws herself on Jesus' feet, with the same complaint that her sister had. Isn't it interesting that Jesus spends time with each sister individually? He could have taught these things to all his disciples and all the Jews who were mourning with the sisters. He could have brought both sisters together first. But he has intimate encounters with each one before entering the house.

Then we read about something that we see Jesus do with only this family. He weeps. There's debate about whether he is weeping over the realities of death and the curse of sin, in sympathy with Mary's grief, or because her and the others' actions reveal that they still don't really get *who he is*. But we see that this scene troubles him. He weeps! And then he shows this family the glory of God by raising their brother from the dead.

One more household scene with Jesus and these siblings reveals, with great intimacy, what they have learned of him (see Matt. 26:6–13; Mark 14:3–9; John 12:1–8). This time Martha is happily serving, Lazarus is reclining with Jesus, and Mary—well, she takes it up a notch! "Mary then took a pound of very costly perfume of pure nard, and anointed the feet of Jesus and wiped His feet with her hair; and the house was filled with the fragrance of the perfume" (John 12:3). These siblings seem to be in sync about enjoying the presence of Jesus and knowing what he has come to do. Martha doesn't complain about Mary's extravagant act—Judas does. By preparing him for burial, Mary shows that she knows the person and the work of Jesus and submits to what he is about to do. And Jesus recognizes this, saying that Mary will be remembered whenever the gospel is preached.

In these accounts, the sisters have all the speaking roles. Clearly Lazarus isn't some passive brother detached from the relationship that his sisters have with Jesus and each other. Jesus calls him a friend. The sisters know of and share in Jesus' love for Lazarus. But it is the sisters' words and actions that God reveals to us in Scripture. We see the fluidity of rights and obligations that we read about in ancient siblingship. We see a quick recovery from rivalry. We see that these siblings treasured one another deeply. As the three of them were oriented toward their relationship with Christ, we see much growth and fruit, which produced harmony in their sibling solidarity.